# NAMING THE SHADOWS

A New Approach to Individual and Group Psychotherapy for
Adult Survivors of Childhood Incest

Susan Roth, Ph.D., and Ronald Batson, M.D.

THE FREE PRESS

New York   London   Toronto   Sydney   Singapore

THE FREE PRESS
A Division of Simon & Schuster
1230 Avenue of the Americas
New York, NY 10020

THE FREE PRESS and colophon are trademarks
of Simon & Schuster Inc.

Manufactured in the United States of America
10 9 8 7 6 5 4 3 2 1

Library of Congress Cataloging-In-Publication Data

Roth, Susan, 1948-
    Naming the shadows : a new approach to individual and group
psychotherapy for adult survivors of childhood incest / Susan Roth
and Ronald Batson.
    p.  cm.
Includes bibliographical references and index.
ISBN: 0-7432-3651-3
1. Incest victims—Rehabilitation.   2. Psychotherapy.   3. Adult
child sexual abuse victims—Rehabilitation.   4. Group psychotherapy.
I. Batson, Ronald.   II. Title.
RC560.I53R684       1997
616.85'83690651—dc21           97-1617
                          CIP

For information regarding special discounts for bulk purchases, please contact Simon &
Schuster Special Sales at 1-800-456-6798 or business@simonandschuster.com

# Contents

# Preface

There is a story by Henry James, which was put to music by Benjamin Britten, about a young girl and boy, Flora and Miles, who are haunted by the years they spent in the care of Miss Jessel, the governess for Flora, and Quint, the manservant for Miles. Miles is the center of the story and of the opera, and his story is all too familiar to those of us who study the abuse of children. Miles is a beautiful, talented, and brilliant youth of 10 who appears to be untouched by an incestuous relationship with his former caretaker, except at those moments when he seems under the power of Quint's ghost. As the story evolves and Miles's current governess becomes aware of the ghost, she at first tries naively to keep Miles from seeing him, hoping to protect Miles from the terror. As the governess realizes that Quint continues to control Miles through his ghost, she tries to help Miles break the secret bond and to destroy Quint's lingering presence. In the end, Quint's power overwhelms the reader as Miles suddenly dies at the moment he speaks the truth about Quint's betrayal.

This particular representation of child abuse is terribly compelling, perhaps partly because it captures the complexity of the experience for a child who suffered intolerable exploitation—as well as for those who tried to help—perhaps partly because we understand something of the horror at the level of our feelings. As social scientists, we believe we have a responsibility to represent this depth, which we have come to understand as psychotherapists, just as we have a responsibility to embrace rules of evidence that ensure the most systematic accumulation of reliable and valid information. It is our intention to hold to this high standard as we describe what we have come to know about dealing with ghosts of the kind Flora and Miles were trapped by.

We began the process of systematically accumulating and appraising information on the psychotherapeutic treatment of adult female survivors of incest in the summer of 1993. As a result of the generous support of the National Institute of Mental Health and the encouragement of their Violence and Traumatic Stress Research Branch, we were able to provide affordable individual and group trauma-focused psychotherapy, as well as pharmacotherapy, over the course of a 12-month period, to six incest survivors. We recorded numerous observations over the course of the year, including periodic responses to standardized clinical assessments, coding of our behavior as therapists, the process of each individual's recovery across sessions, and the interaction of group members during therapy sessions. Our observations during the course of this study, and the intellectual exchange they generated between us and with our students, greatly sharpened our accumulated knowledge over many years of clinical service and scholarship on the psychotherapeutic treatment for women sexually abused as children by family members.

If one considers reducing representations of human suffering to quantifiable forms, or characterizing in some orderly fashion the intimate communication of psychotherapy that often occurs on a number of different levels simultaneously, one immediately appreciates the challenge of putting forward psychotherapy as a science. To meet this challenge, we will rely on our deeply ingrained skills of abstracting generalizations from observations across subjects, as well as on the presentation of qualitative data, scientific storytelling if you will, to stay true to the complexity and subjectivity of the individuals we have studied. We aim to present more a point of view than a recipe to guide others in understanding the process of coping with childhood sexual abuse.

Facing the reality of incest takes strength and courage on the part of the survivor and creative balance on the part of the therapist; the collaboration must establish a context in which the survivor can experience the emotional intensity and meaning of victimization, while at the same time experiencing herself in relation to others in a way that is self-enhancing. While survivors often do not hold their abuse clearly in mind, the memory haunts them. The therapeutic relationship provides the context that allows a state of mind where one can more tolerably come to know what has been lost from focus, a state of mind where a thoughtful, reflective construction of information is possible. As our clients have taught us, things as mysterious or ephemeral as ghosts often "clarify" as an evolving narrative of childhood abuse.

# Acknowledgments

This book grew out of a collaboration that began in June of 1990 when our common expertise in working with adult survivors of childhood incest led to an initial meeting. While we had both been living in the Raleigh–Durham–Chapel Hill Triangle area for many years before that, our paths had not crossed sooner, owing to our different professional backgrounds and commitments. It was not long after our meeting that we discovered that we were of like minds in how we thought about the problems trauma survivors faced and about the best way to approach these problems in psychotherapy. Our regular discussions over the next 6 years, prior to the completion of the book, involved an exciting intellectual exchange that blurred the boundaries of psychiatry and psychology, the domains of the clinician and researcher, and the limits of our own ideas. We began the actual research project that is the basis for the current book in the summer of 1993.

Dr. Susan Roth is responsible for the development, design, and conduct of the group treatment. This treatment was developed at the Duke University Psychology Training Clinic, and Dr. Roth would like to acknowledge the contributions to this effort of her former students, most notably Leslie Lebowitz, Ph.D., and Elana Newman, Ph.D. Dr. Roth also had oversight of the design and funding of

*Acknowledgments*

the research project and would like to thank students Ruth DeRosa, Ph.D., and Kiban Turner for their efforts in the research process. They are largely responsible for the collection and preparation of the quantitative data reported in chapter 3. In addition, their observations of and assistance with the group therapy process contributed to Dr. Roth's preparation of case material drawn from the group treatment. Thanks are due also to Jonathan Davidson, M.D., for the productive years of research collaboration that encompassed the research project reported here, and to Susan Solomon, Ph.D., at the National Institute of Health for her encouragement and support.

Dr. Roth, who did the actual writing of the book, is grateful to Duke University for providing a sabbatical leave, and to Princeton University for providing a teaching opportunity that made it possible to write while looking south to the Empire State Building and west to the Hudson River in the city she loves. Dr. Roth is also grateful to Philip Rappaport at The Free Press for believing in the book from the start and for making it extremely easy to enter the world of book publishing. On a more personal note, Dr. Roth would like to warmly acknowledge her teachers, Richard Bootzin, Ph.D., and Kenneth Howard, Ph.D., and her colleagues at Duke, Philip Costanzo, Ph.D., Irving Alexander, Ph.D., and John Coie, Ph.D., for their friendship and intellectual guidance over the years. Also, without the support of friends and colleagues in the International Society for Traumatic Stress Studies there would be no context for this work. Thanks especially to Elizabeth Brett, Ph.D., Edna Foa, Ph.D., Bonnie Green, Ph.D., Terence Keane, Ph.D., Leslie Lebowitz, Ph.D., David Lisak, Ph.D., Susan Solomon, Ph.D., and Bessel van der Kolk, M.D. Finally, Dr. Roth would like to dedicate this book to her husband, Philip Costanzo, and her son, Anthony Roth Costanzo, without whose love this work would not have been possible.

Dr. Ronald Batson is responsible for the development, design,

*Acknowledgments*

and conduct of the individual treatment and has conveyed through extensive oral discussions and written descriptions the complex, and at times elusive, nature of the individual psychotherapy. Dr. Batson would like to thank his many teachers who have prompted his learning. In this regard, he wants to especially acknowledge the important influence that Elaine Carmen, M.D., has had on his interest in, and understanding of, psychological trauma. He has also appreciated the helpful curiosity and encouragement of his close colleagues, Fred Irons, M.D., and Pat Moore, M.D., during the course of this study. In addition, Dr. Batson wishes to acknowledge the support of Philip Costanzo, Ph.D., in his work at Duke University. He is grateful to his inquisitive students at the Duke University Psychology Training Clinic and previously at University of North Carolina Hospitals, for the opportunity to evolve his ideas by "thinking out loud" with them. He would like to thank Richard Gess not only for his specific assistance on this project but also for his contribution to Dr. Batson's understanding of evocative language and communication over the many years of their collaboration. Finally, Dr. Batson offers a special thanks to his wife, Janet Morris-Batson, and his son, Evan Davis Batson, for their kind and patient support.

We are both grateful to the people we have treated in psychotherapy over the years, especially Alice, Annie, Caroline, Ceci, Jesse, and Jo, for teaching us what we know.

*Chapter* 1

# Special Considerations
# in Treating Incest Survivors

The purpose of our book is to provide a systematic and richly descriptive account of our treatment approach for adult survivors of childhood incest. We hope the book will be of interest to both academic and nonacademic clinicians and their trainees, as well as to adult survivors of incest who are not therapists. Although our work is built around the presentation of quantitative data and extensive case material on six *female* survivors of childhood incest, we believe our approach is applicable to male survivors as well and represents an orientation to individual and group psychotherapy that is broadly useful in the treatment of all trauma survivors.

Much of what we do as therapists depends on our conceptualization of what it is we are trying to treat. In opening our psychotherapeutic work to public view, one of our goals is to show the complexity of the psychological lives of survivors of familial sexual abuse and to establish due respect for the challenges this complexity presents in the treatment process. In this first chapter, we intend to make a strong case for targeting issues of identity and relatedness when providing psychotherapy for incest survivors. The symptoms of posttraumatic stress disorder (PTSD) have become an important treatment focus for trauma survivors in general, critically locating survivors' problems in the traumatic exposure, and while these symptoms are an important target of treatment for incest survivors, we do not believe they should be the *exclusive* focus of treatment.

An important premise of our work is that incest occurs in a larger social context that can be defined by lack of protection. We conceptualize the long-term psychological sequelae of incest as an *adaptation* to this larger social context of childhood family life, an adaptation that disrupts the normative developmental processes of defining, regulating, and integrating aspects of the self and of meaningfully relating to others in a secure way. Thus identity and relational issues in adult survivors derive, in our view, from an enduring adaptation to childhood trauma.

In this chapter, we describe the ways that we have defined the targets of our treatment, and we anchor this description in two ways. First we contextualize our own work by a brief discussion of the empirical and theoretical literature on the long-term sequela of childhood sexual abuse, noting the recent trends in conceptualization that echo our own interests. Then we orient our readers toward the words of our subjects as well as to characters of fiction who represent the experience of our subjects. We do the latter in order to evoke a more intuitive and emotional understanding, which we believe is extremely important to keep in mind.

Our emphases in this chapter on the construction of traumatic meaning and on traumatic states of mind continues throughout the book and highlights our psychotherapeutic approach. We believe the individual and group psychotherapies create an alternative social context that allows for bringing into focus an ever-present but overlooked trauma memory that exists in revivifications and adaptive transformations of traumatic experience. As trauma-driven experience becomes open to the influence of the therapeutic process, the pride to value oneself in relationships is gained through self-knowledge derived from a reflective appraisal of the lingering influence of childhood abuse.

## Posttraumatic Sequelae of Childhood Sexual Abuse

Since Diana Russell's groundbreaking article, "The Incidence and Prevalence of Intrafamilial and Extrafamilial Sexual Abuse of Female Children," in 1983, social scientists have firmly established with increasingly sophisticated methods that childhood sexual abuse occurs fairly commonly (e.g., see Finkelhor, Hotaling, Lewis & Smith, 1990; Saunders, Villeponteauz, Lipovsky, Kilpatrick & Veronen, 1992). Over approximately the last 15 years, data have also been accumulating that attest to the enduring and negative psychological impact of this form of child maltreatment. While the empirical literature does not routinely treat different categories of childhood sexual abuse separately, there is a consistent understanding by researchers that sexual abuse that occurs within the family context is likely to produce more complicated problems. Incest by a father, for example, is rarely a discrete traumatic event, represents a profound disturbance in a primary relationship, and lasts longer than some other forms of child sexual abuse because of the insular nature of the family (Cole & Putnam, 1992). In the past decade, there has also been a proliferation of clinical literature relevant to the treatment of adult survivors of childhood incest (Briere, 1989, 1992; Courtois, 1988; Herman, 1992; Horowitz, 1986; Kluft, 1989, 1990; Ochberg, 1988; Ochberg & Willis, 1991; Roth, DeRosa & Turner, 1996; Spiegel, 1989; Spiegel & Cardena, 1990; van der Kolk, 1987).

The empirical literature on the posttraumatic sequelae of childhood sexual abuse includes studies of children who have been sexually abused as well as studies of adults who were sexually abused as children. In both cases, researchers have focused on psychological *symptoms and disorders* that correlate with the experience of childhood sexual abuse (for reviews of this literature, see Browne & Finkelhor, 1986; Cole & Putnam, 1992; Kendall-Tackett, Williams & Finkelhor, 1993; Polusny & Follette, 1995).

In the literature describing the impact of sexual abuse on children, studies are easily organized around symptoms, including anxiety, fear, posttraumatic stress disorder, depression, somatic complaints, aggression, sexualized behavior, learning problems, behavior problems, and self-destructive behavior. In fact, Kendall-Tackett et al. (1993, p. 173) conclude that, "there is virtually no general domain of symptomatology that has not been associated with a history of sexual abuse." They note at the same time, however, that both sexualized behavior and symptoms of posttraumatic stress disorder occur with relatively high frequency and appear to be the only two groups of symptoms more common in sexually abused children than in other clinical groups. As these reviewers and others have noted, most studies are atheoretical and simply describe characteristics of children who have been sexually abused.

Studies of adults are also largely atheoretical, attempting to describe characteristics of survivors, or trying to determine if a history of childhood sexual abuse is more common among certain clinical groups (Cole & Putnam, 1992; Polusny & Follette, 1995). The expected high frequency of posttraumatic stress disorder among adult survivors, concern with problems relating to sexuality, including high-risk sexual behaviors, and problems with sexual satisfaction and adjustment all echo the findings with children. Also consistent with the research on children, however, is the impressive *range* of symptoms found to correlate with a history of childhood sexual abuse, including symptoms of other anxiety disorders, depression, substance abuse, eating disorders, dissociative disorders, somatoform disorders, and personality disorders such as self-harming behaviors. Finally, in addition to looking at correlates of child sexual abuse within a context of traditional diagnostic categories, there has been an examination of broad-based social and relational functioning, including revictimization, which again shows adult survivors of childhood sexual abuse to be at risk for the development of negative adult outcomes.

In Judith Herman's description of child abuse in her outstanding book, *Trauma and Recovery* (1992), she begins with the premise that child victims of sexual abuse within the family must adapt to an ongoing situation that is truly intolerable. This adaptation will necessarily be extraordinary if one is to survive psychologically.

> The child trapped in an abusive environment is faced with formidable tasks of adaptation. She must find a way to preserve a sense of trust in people who are untrustworthy, safety in a situation that is unsafe, control in a situation that is terrifyingly unpredictable, power in a situation of helplessness. . . . The pathological environment of childhood abuse forces the development of extraordinary capacities, both creative and destructive. It fosters the development of abnormal states of consciousness in which the ordinary relations of body and mind, reality and imagination, knowledge and memory, no longer hold. These altered states of consciousness permit the elaboration of a prodigious array of symptoms, both somatic and psychological. And these symptoms simultaneously conceal and reveal their origins; they speak in disguised language of secrets too terrible for words. (p. 96)

Like Herman, Pamela Cole and Frank Putnam (1992), in an attempt to synthesize the empirical work on the immediate and long-term effects of incest, argue that the diverse and nonspecific effects of child sexual abuse reflect an underlying organization of interference with self and social development. According to Cole and Putnam, incest interferes with developmental transitions, each of which is associated with revision in one's self-definition and integration, in the regulation of behavior and affect, and in the scope and quality of one's social relationships. The incest experience interferes with these necessary developmental transitions in a manner that increases the risk of serious psychopathology.

There are a number of explicit and implicit points here that are important assumptions in our own work and that we would like to emphasize. First, while it is true that a wide array of symptoms and disorders are likely correlates of childhood sexual abuse, there is something lost in treating those symptoms without some understanding of their relationship to a traumatic adaptation. Second, the complex adaptation to trauma necessary in cases of ongoing, familial sexual abuse requires a distortion of reality that often involves the recruitment of altered states of consciousness. Third, the complex adaptation to trauma necessarily disrupts normative self and social development, making issues of identity and relatedness important targets for psychotherapeutic treatment.

## The Targets of Treatment

In the systematic study of posttraumatic sequela and their treatment, we believe that a number of factors have recently converged on a consensus to conceptualize targets of treatment complexly, particularly for those interpersonal traumas that occur early on and chronically in the context of family life. One factor is the avowed desirability of narrowing the clinician-researcher gap by bringing into the researcher's domain more difficult-to-measure phenomena that are familiar to the clinician. Another is the appeal of developmental models that necessarily emphasize the theoretical underpinnings of disordered behavior. A third factor is the growing influence of narrative methodology, which focuses on the meanings that people give their lives, and the ways in which they actively and privately construct their experience. A final component is the current respectability of recruiting constructs relating to variable states of consciousness, or states of mind, for understanding how children survive unlivable circumstances of family life. These factors have influenced the development of a number of distinctive approaches to representing the impact of trauma that are important in our work and that we describe below. The approaches all derive from clinical observation, but otherwise they vary considerably in their relationship to traditional diagnostic approaches and their ease of measurement. They all suggest treatment targets in addition to PTSD as essential considerations in treatment planning for adult survivors of incest. For now, we simply describe the three distinctive approaches and ask for the reader's patience as their relationship to one another and to our treatment unfolds over the remaining chapters.

## Complex Posttraumatic Stress Disorder: An Emerging Diagnosis

In preparation for the fourth edition of the *Diagnostic and Statistical Manual of the American Psychiatric Association* (1994), the DSM-IV, a systematic study of a large clinical sample as well as a smaller but randomly generated community sample was designed to address certain issues with regard to the DSM-IIIR diagnosis of posttraumatic stress disorder (Davidson & Foa, 1992; Kilpatrick, Resnick, Freedy, Pelcovitz, Resick, Roth & van der Kolk, 1997). This study is referred to as the PTSD Field Trial, and one of its aims was to investige a constellation of trauma-related symptoms not addressed by the PTSD diagnosis. This constellation of symptoms was observed with great consistency by clinician-scholars working with certain trauma populations, such as those exposed to prolonged, repeated abuse (see Herman, 1992; Pelcovitz, van der Kolk, Roth, Mandel, Kaplan & Resick,

1997; van der Kolk, Pelcovitz, Roth, Mandel, McFarlane & Herman, 1996). Although this "complex posttraumatic stress disorder," as named by Herman, had not been systematically studied before, trauma researchers had for some time debated the adequacy of PTSD as a description of the psychological sequelae of certain kinds of traumatic exposure, and had considered providing an additional formulation relating to trauma within the standard diagnostic nomenclature (see Pelcovitz et al., 1997).

The notion of a complex posttraumatic stress *disorder* is still controversial today, and the symptoms of Complex PTSD defined in the DSM-IV Field Trial presently appear in the DSM-IV as *associated features* of PTSD. As work evolves in this area, it is useful for clinicians and researchers alike to be aware of the current knowledge base, as it has substantial relevance, in our view, to the design of psychotherapeutic interventions for incest survivors. For those readers not familiar with the simple PTSD diagnosis, we have presented in tabular form (see Table 1–1) a definition of each of the three categories of PTSD symptoms (American Psychiatric Association, 1994).

DEFINITION AND MEASUREMENT OF COMPLEX PTSD. As described by Pelcovitz et al. (1997), two independent groups of clinician-researchers in Boston and New York delineated a cluster of symptoms observed in response to extreme trauma that formed the basis of the clinical interview used in the field trial to gather information about seven categories of symptoms comprising Complex PTSD (see Table 1–2). This structured interview (van der Kolk, Pelcovitz, Herman, Roth, Kaplan & Spitzer, 1992) was reliably administered by expert clinicians at the five different research sites for the field trial, although substantial experience with trauma populations was required to make difficult clinical judgments. Data from 520 subjects resulted in the formulation of Complex PTSD which is outlined in Table 1–2.

**TABLE 1–1**

*Definition of Simple Posttraumatic Stress Disorder Symptoms*

---

**Intrusive** *symptoms* describe a persistent reexperiencing of trauma in the form of recurrent and intrusive distressing recollections, recurrent distressing dreams, a sense of reliving traumatic experience as in dissociative (flashback) episodes, and intense psychological or physiological distress at exposure to events that symbolize or resemble an aspect of the traumatic experience.

**Avoidant** *symptoms* include persistent avoidance of stimuli associated with the traumatic experience, or numbing of responsiveness associated with the traumatic experience. Deliberate efforts to avoid associated thoughts, feelings, activities, and situations that might call the traumatic experience to mind, an inability to recall aspects of the traumatic experience, a markedly diminished interest in significant activities, feelings of detachment or estrangement from others, a restricted range of feelings, including, for example, the inability to have loving feelings, and the sense of a foreshortened future are all symptoms included in this category.

**Hyperarousal** *symptoms* include persistent symptoms of increased arousal, such as difficulty falling or staying asleep, irritability or outbursts of anger, difficulty concentrating, hypervigilance, and exaggerated startling.

---

The seven symptom categories described by Complex PTSD are consistent with the notion of a traumatic adaptation that disrupts important developmental processes. Affect regulation (IA), for example, refers to an inability to find nondestructive ways of calming oneself down when upset, a problem that is judged to result from the impact of trauma on normative developmental achievements. Permanent damage (IIIB), as another example, refers to a person's sense of there being something wrong that can't be fixed as a result of traumatic life experiences. Preliminary data from the field trial on reliability and validity as well as more recent data attest to the value of continued research of the Complex PTSD cluster and to its clinical utility (see Newman, Orsillo, Herman, Niles & Litz, 1995; Newman, Riggs & Roth, 1997; Pelcovitz et al., 1997; Roth, Newman,

**TABLE 1–2**

*Symptom Categories and Diagnostic Criteria for Complex PTSD*

## I. Alterations in Regulation of Affect and Impulses

A. Affect regulation  
B. Modulation of anger  
C. Self-destructive  

D. Suicidal preoccupation  
E. Difficulty modulating sexual involvement  
F. Excessive risk taking  

*A and one of B–F required*

## II. Alterations in Attention or Consciousness

A. Amnesia  
B. Transient dissociative episodes and depersonalization  

*A or B required*

## III. Alterations in Self-Perception

A. Ineffectiveness  
B. Permanent damage  
C. Guilt and responsibility  

D. Shame  
E. Nobody can understand  
F. Minimizing  

*Two of A–F required*

## IV. Alterations in Perception of the Perpetrator

A. Adopting distorted beliefs  
B. Idealization of the perpetrator  

C. Preoccupation with hurting perpetrator  

*Not required*

## V. Alterations in Relations with Others

A. Inability to trust  
B. Revictimization  

C. Victimizing others  

*One of A–C required*

## VI. Somatization

A. Digestive system  
B. Chronic pain  
C. Cardiopulmonary symptoms  

D. Conversion symptoms  
E. Sexual symptoms  

*Two of A–E required*

## VII. Alterations in Systems of Meaning

A. Despair and hopelessness  

B. Loss of previously sustaining beliefs  

*A or B required*

*Source:* Pelcovitz et al., 1997.

*Special Considerations in Treating Incest Survivors*

Pelcovitz, van der Kolk & Mandel, 1996; van der Kolk, Dreyfus, Michaels, Shera, Berkowitz, Fisler & Saxe, 1994; van der Kolk, Pelcovitz & Roth, 1993; van der Kolk et al., 1996). Its utility is bolstered further by the inclusion of a similar diagnosis into the ICD-10 nomenclature, "Enduring Personality Change After Catastrophic Experience" (World Health Organization, 1994).

COMPLEX PTSD IN SUBJECTS EXPOSED TO SEXUAL ABUSE. Working with the field trial data, Roth, Newman, Pelcovitz, van der Kolk, and Mandel (1996) looked at the clinical relevance of Complex PTSD for sexually and physically abused subjects. One hundred sixty-seven sexually abused subjects, who were predominantly female (approximately 90%), were categorized according to whether their abuse was acute (single event) or chronic (2 years or more), and according to whether the abuse started before or after age 13. Just over 50% of the sexually abused subjects had been chronically abused, and for almost 70% of these subjects the abuse had an early onset. Chronicity was related to the rate of occurrence of Complex PTSD, and fully 76% of the sexually abused subjects who carried a lifetime diagnosis of PTSD also carried a lifetime diagnosis of complex PTSD (as compared with 53% of the physically abused subjects). These data argue strongly for targeting this broader conceptualization of posttraumatic sequela in the psychotherapeutic treatment of adult survivors of childhood sexual abuse.

BORDERLINE PERSONALITY DISORDER AS ANOTHER LAYER OF SEVERITY. The relationship between posttraumatic stress disorder and borderline personality disorder (BPD) has become a highly debated topic (see DeRosa, Roth, Newman, Pelcovitz & van der Kolk, 1997), with discussions focusing on the overlap of the two disorders and the role of chronic childhood sexual trauma in BPD (e.g., see Herman & van der Kolk, 1987). Of course, the introduction of complex posttraumatic stress disorder potentially complicates the picture, given the evident similarities in symptoms between Complex PTSD and borderline personality disorder. At the Duke site of the field trial, where the first author was the investigator, additional data on borderline personality disorder were collected on 74 subjects (see DeRosa et al., 1997).

The data suggest an extension of the argument put forward in the field trial for the relationship found between simple and complex PTSD; patients with Complex PTSD were considered to represent the more severely affected PTSD patients. This conclusion was supported by two findings: The vast majority of people with Complex PTSD also suffered from PTSD, and only a subset of the people with PTSD carried a Complex PTSD diagnosis. In a similar manner, the current data suggest that patients with borderline personality disorder represent the more severely affected Complex PTSD patients. Again, this conclusion is supported by two findings: The vast majority of people with BPD also suffered from Complex PTSD, and only a subset of the people with Complex PTSD also carried a BPD diagnosis. Perhaps this layered structure is the best way to conceptualize the relationship among these three trauma-related disorders. Interestingly, as the severity of diagnosis increases, histories of childhood trauma are more prevalent. For example, of the people meeting diagnositic criteria for both Complex PTSD and borderline personality disorder, 75% had childhood histories of physical and/or sexual abuse, more than twice as many as in the Simple PTSD group.

The implication of these findings for our treatment is in its limits or boundaries in terms of whom we believe we can safely treat within the time frame used in our current work. While we do not explicitly exclude people from treatment who meet criteria for borderline personality disorder, we do have certain exclusion criteria that overlap with the BPD diagnosis and that effectively exclude people in all but the mild range of the disorder. We are treating a very different population of survivors than is Marsha Linehan (1993), for example. They are adult survivors of incest who are likely in the midrange of severity in terms of the impact of the traumatic exposure. A fuller description of our treatment sample appears in chapter 3.

## Thematic Assessment

It is currently acceptable to argue, as a social scientist, that people actively construct their experience and that this complex process results in representations of the self, others, and the world more generally. It is also well accepted among the community of scholars who study people exposed to traumatic events that such exposure is an extraordinary experience that challenges the representational process, disorganizing personality in the worst case and routinely demanding an integration of emotionally intense meanings. At the most basic level, the construction of experience, or the ongoing process of symbolizing experience in a meaningful way, is essential for psychological well-being. It is as part of this process that particular "traumatic" meanings or constructions of traumatic experience evolve over time, characterizing a dynamic adaptation that is a critical focus for trauma scholars and clinicians. The measurement of these meanings—what we refer to as *thematic assessment*—is a kind of assessment that has been gaining in popularity in recent years as a way of representing the effects of trauma, tapping into a clinically significant traumatic process, and allowing for the articulation of targets of therapeutic change separate from symptoms of disorder (see Roth, Lebowitz & DeRosa, 1996).

While the evaluation of traumatic meanings has substantial conceptual overlap with the evaluation of some of the Complex PTSD symptoms, thematic assessment derives from a very different scholarly tradition that is central in our work and perhaps closer to our hearts than psychiatric diagnostic models. Some of the important assumptions we hold in our work are best illustrated by a brief description of Seymore Epstein's cognitive-experiential self-theory (1994), which follows. We then describe the trauma themes we target in our psychotherapy and summarize some of the background research done over the past 10 years or so at Duke University. Finally, we present an illustration of the rich, narrative material we have relied on in systematically developing these treatment targets. As will become clear, trauma themes represent complex and often difficult-to-measure aspects of an adaptation to traumatic experience that continues to drive experience in the present.

COGNITIVE-EXPERIENTIAL SELF-THEORY. A number of different traditions within psychology and psychiatry have converged on the same perspective, which is that the essence of the traumatic process lies in the recovery from an invalidation or preemption of healthy fundamental beliefs or schemata (see Roth, Lebowitz & DeRosa, 1996). We have chosen to focus our discussion on Epstein's articulation of this point of view because central aspects of his orientation are most consistent with our own orientation. Although there are multiple levels of consciousness considered in his theory, there is an emphasis on the preconscious, on an experiential system that is no less wise or adaptive than the rational mind, and on an emotional system that is neither subsumed under rational constructions nor separate from cognitive processes.

Epstein (1994) presents compelling evidence that people apprehend reality in two fundamentally different ways: one intuitive, narrative, experiential; the other analytical, deliberate, and rational. His cognitive-experiential self-theory argues for the existence of two major adaptive systems, an experiential system and a rational system, both of which organize experience and direct behavior. It is the experiential system that is assumed to be associated with affect, and thus with a different mode of processing information or of knowing than the rational system. Epstein describes the experiential system, for example, as "experienced passively and preconsciously: we are seized by our emotions," in contrast to the rational system as, "experienced actively and consciously: we are in control of our thoughts." Likewise, the experiential system is, "self-evidently valid: experiencing is believing," where the rational system, "requires justification via logic and evidence" (p. 711). Importantly for our purpose of considering thematic assessment, the experiential system encodes reality in metaphors and narratives and derives knowledge that is often more compelling and more likely to influence behavior. At its higher reaches, and particularly in interaction with the rational system, it is a source of intuitive wisdom and creativity.

According to cognitive-experiential self-theory (CEST), people have constructs about the self and the world in both the experiential and rational systems. In contrast to *beliefs* in the rational system, there are implicit beliefs or schemata in the experiential system that include generalizations from emotionally significant past experiences, which are organized into an overall system and are subject to disorganization following unassimilable emotional experiences. Generalizations and abstractions in the experiential system result from the use of prototypes, metaphors, scripts, and narratives. Although the experiential and rational systems are reciprocally influential, the experiential system is assumed to be dominant over the rational system because it is less effortful, is likely to be experienced as more compelling because of its association with affect, and is difficult to control because its influence is usually outside of awareness. Cognitive-experiential self-theory assumes there is a ubiquitous influence of automatic thinking outside of awareness on conscious thinking and behavior.

According to CEST (Epstein, 1991, 1994), a preconscious theory of reality determines to a large extent how a person perceives, thinks, feels, and behaves. Behavior is determined by the joint influence of the need to maximize pleasure and minimize pain, the need to maintain a coherent and stable conceptual system, the need for relatedness, and the need to enhance self-esteem. Associated with these needs or basic functions of a personal theory of reality are four basic beliefs: (a) a belief regarding the benevolence of the world, (b) a belief that the world is meaningful, (c) a belief that people are trustworthy and worth relating to, and (d) a belief that the self is worthy. As a result of exposure to traumatic experiences, the basic constructs or beliefs are threatened at a deep experiential level, and the individual must reestablish stability by modifying fundamental beliefs to accommodate the traumatic experiences.

There is a fundamental motive to assimilate representations of emotionally significant experiences into a coherent, unified conceptual system. This is adaptive because it promotes the construction of a coherent model of the world that is consistent with experience. When material cannot be assimilated because its emotional significance is intolerable or because it is so discrepant with fundamental schemata, it is dissociated in some way. Compulsive repetitions in memory, for example, are abortive attempts at assimilation. According to CEST, psychotherapy must affect the experiential system, which it can accomplish in one of three ways: (a) using the rational system to influence the experiential system; (b) teaching directly from emotionally significant experiences, such as constructive relationships with significant others, including therapists; and (c) communicating with the experiential system in its own medium, namely what Epstein calls fantasy.

TRAUMA THEMES. As noted by Roth, Lebowitz & DeRosa (1996), feminists and other social scientists working to expand our current knowledge base have put forward compelling arguments for the

*Special Considerations in Treating Incest Survivors*

methodological importance of open and semistructured interviews and of narrative, thematic analysis. The belief that interviewing and the analysis of narrative is central to creating new bodies of more inclusive and accurate information is so fundamental to radical social scientists that it cuts across disciplinary lines and is gaining momentum and acceptance generally as a legitimate methodology. The use of this narrative methodology gives the research subject the power to define what is important to study in a context that is naturally conducive to the emergence of meaningful information, even of the sort that is less readily accessible, that is, less conscious or less socially supported.

Our work at Duke on trauma themes (see especially Roth & Batson, 1993; Roth & Lebowitz, 1988; Roth & Newman, 1992, 1993; Roth, Lebowitz & DeRosa, 1996) began with the work described in Roth and Lebowitz, which was based on unstructured interviews with treatment-seeking survivors of a variety of sexual traumas (e.g., adult date rape, adult stranger rape, childhood incest). Subjects were asked to present their story of what had happened and what it had meant to them, and from these data, themes relating to difficulties in coping were abstracted and organized into conceptually coherent and clinically meaningful categories.

These themes have since been studied with narrative material in various contexts, with the goal of understanding how individuals process traumatic material over time as they move toward resolution of traumatic meanings. Although our coding system is complex and difficult to learn (see Lifton, Newman, Lebowitz & Roth, 1996), there is substantial evidence that the themes capture the complex coping process we had hoped to characterize. An illustration of what we consider to be a rich, descriptive account of the processing of traumatic themes over the course of therapy appears below. Table 1–3 includes the actual names of our themes and a summary of how

**TABLE 1–3**

*Summary of Trauma Themes and Thematic Resolution*

THEMES

*Helplessness*—e.g., a feeling that someone else has absolute power over you

*Rage*—e.g., a feeling that your rage will be emotionally overwhelming

*Fear*—e.g., behavior that is phobic and protective

*Loss*—e.g., a feeling that a traumatic experience stole something from you

*Shame*—e.g., feelings of humiliation for having been exposed to sexual abuse

*Alienation*—e.g., a feeling of being different and set apart from other people

*Benign/Meaningful World*—e.g., a belief that the world is dangerous, unrewarding and/or unjust

*People Trustworthy*—e.g., an expectation of others being unhelpful, capable of deception, betrayal, and exploitation

*Self-Worthy*—e.g., a sense of being flawed or damaged

*Self-Blame/Guilt*—a belief or feeling that you are in some way responsible for abuse perpetrated against you

*Reciprocity*—e.g., a feeling of being unworthy of receiving love

*Legitimacy*—e.g., a feeling of being deviant in your reaction to sexual abuse

*(continued)*

we represent thematic resolution. In the work with trauma themes, we have argued that the survivor must come to understand the emotional impact of traumatic experiences so that she is no longer preoccupied or driven by negative feelings, and that she must grapple with the meaning of traumatic experiences until an adaptive resolution is achieved. The essence of an adaptive resolution, after Epstein (1991), is the modification or accommodation of the belief system in a manner that both incorporates the trauma and permits realistic coping with and enjoyment of life, while recognizing its limitations. Maladaptive schematic resolutions tend to maintain a chronic state of negative affect and provide an excessively restric-

*Special Considerations in Treating Incest Survivors*

**TABLE 1-3** *(continued)*

---

### DIMENSIONS OF RESOLUTION

---

1. *No Conscious Awareness*—e.g., a subject describes interpersonal encounters that suggest an extreme lack of trust of others, without in any way acknowledging that this is an issue

2. *Tentative Movement Toward Acknowledgment*—e.g., a subject describes avoiding TV if the story involves a child losing something or someone important to her

3. *General Acknowledgment*—e.g., a subject states that she feels poisonous some of the time, and very different from other people most of the time

4. *Awareness of Association with Trauma*—e.g., a subject describes how she should have done something to keep her father from abusing her, and how her lack of action makes her culpable

5. *Attempt Resolution*—e.g., a subject decides to talk with her mother about what her father did to her in the hope that her mother will absolve her of some of her guilt

6. *Resolution*—e.g., a subject describes how she's learned to discriminate trustworthy from untrustworthy men

---

tive and biased way of relating to the world. One purpose of psychotherapy is to process these thematic issues. Survivors are, for example, helped to understand the feelings they have surrounding traumatic experiences, many of which they do not initially connect to trauma or are even aware of consciously. They are also helped to understand what significance traumatic experiences have for their view of themselves, others, and the world more generally, and to consider alternative views as a result of other life experiences and their experience in therapy.

NARRATIVE ILLUSTRATION: JACKIE (see Roth & Newman, 1993). Jackie is a 25-year-old bright, articulate, white college student who believed at the start of treatment that both her father and her uncle had sexually abused her, although she had no cohesive traumatic memories. At an interview 3 months into treatment, Jackie spoke quite a bit about her sense of responsibility for the abuse she had experienced. Most noteworthy in her narrative is the fact that in talking about self-blame, she also speaks about violation and powerlessness, and offers the idea that her sense of responsibility keeps her from her anger and fear:

*From what I can understand, my dad would do whatever he did to me, then I'd leave the room and they [her family] would tell me that I was horrible and disgusting in ways like they'd watch me or talk out loud with each other, but about, not to, me, but I'd be standing right there. And then I carried that attitude to school and feel like I'm being judged by people the same way I've been judged by my family all my life. I must have thought I'm this horrible, disgusting, leprosy kind of person. Why? I know why. It's 'cause, who would do a thing like what I did [referring to having sex with her father]?*

*It's like I feel like I brought on what happened to me by being sexual. When I see somebody else acting like that [sexual], I feel threatened by the person because I feel like they're taking away attention from me. And the other side of it is, the attention I'm assuming is being given her, which is similar to what was given to me as a kid, is violating her. Raping her with their eyes. And when I see a girl getting violated that way, I feel like I'm being violated. And that feeling gets me so frustrated, my reaction is to want to take off my clothes, rip them off and throw myself out in the middle of the road and say fuck you to everybody. And the feeling I think is the frustration of the powerlessness. I tried so hard to control what parts of my body I give, whether visually or physically, and not being able to do it with my father and the other people who were around, or with other people in public when I assume they're violating me visually . . . I feel like I'm trying so hard to be in control and contain myself, keep myself private [yet I still feel like] I'm being taken from.*

*It's very difficult to get me pissed because I blame everything on*

*Special Considerations in Treating Incest Survivors*

me. . . . *One thing that I can't accept is the fact that I think I liked it [the incest] and enjoyed it, and then it started getting bad. Like I think the physical contact felt good at first and then it got a little bit too much for me and I felt horrible, guilty, gross, and disgusting, but I denied it because I didn't want to lose the good part. I don't know exactly if there was a point where I wanted to stop and couldn't or what, but the initial part of that makes it seem to me more like I did a guilty thing rather than I was a badly abused, afraid, little girl. Now an afraid little girl I can accept and feel good about. But a guilty thing 'cause I did something bad, I can't accept. I don't know, sometimes I have a lot of fear, and then sometimes I have just a lot of guilt.*

At an interview 9 months into treatment, it is clear that Jackie's sense of power has changed considerably, and this change is reflected in her insights about helplessness and in her behavior toward one of her childhood perpetrators:

*All of a sudden I feel like somebody is going to get me. Or if I have to deal with people in a professional level, I'm afraid they're going to get me. But now I recognize that the reason I feel that way is because that's how I associate my perpetrators [as] these older authority men. And whenever I get in contact with older authority men I feel their power. And now that I recognize that, all I have to do is tell myself, "I'm an adult and that's not true, and I can take care of myself," and all that stuff. And I feel better. So that's why I don't feel helpless.*

*When I went over there to his [uncle's] office, I went over there with Don [boyfriend], and the three of us were standing, at one point, behind this desk. And Fred had to leave the room, and on his way out, he rubbed my ass from one side to the other very carefully with his hand. And I just stood there kind of in shock. You know, "Did that really happen?" And he left the room and I told Don that I realized that my sixth sense told me that I had to confront him with that, at least, to break the cycle, to show whoever inside of me thinks I'm powerless that I'm not. But I was scared to death to do it. And I knew I had to do it alone. So when Fred came back in the room it was planned that Don would leave. And I told him, "I would appreciate it if you would never touch my body again anywhere unless you had my permission." And he said that he didn't know what I was talking about, that he didn't remember touching my body. So I told him when and how it happened. And I said, "If you really don't remember doing it, then maybe that's something you should look at, because it's not very good for you to be going around doing those kind of things and not remembering them." He proceeded to play all the games he probably played when I was a little girl. He said he's been going out of his way to do nice things for me, but he's losing his patience. It was a threat. He is the controller of the money I get, all my income. I finally said, "Look, I don't think we're having trouble understanding each other. I think we just disagree. If you'd like at some later date, we can get back together again and talk about this, but for right now, I'd like to get home." And he said, "No, I'd rather just throw it out the window right now and bury it." And inside I said, "I bet you would." And that was it.*

### The Adaptational Blueprint

The general recognition of dissociative aspects of many posttraumatic psychiatric sequelae has resulted in efforts to identify common psychological processes across trauma-related disorders, and to implicate these processes in treatment (Batson, 1992, 1994; Bernstein & Putnam, 1986; Putnam, 1989; Spiegel, 1989; Spiegel & Cardena, 1990, 1991; van der Kolk & Fisler, 1995; van der Kolk et al., 1996). In the current academic discourse by experts in the field of dissociation, there is agreement that people who suffer from dissociative identity disorder (formerly called multiple personality disorder) represent the extreme on a continuum of severity, and that the condition is often reflective of early, severe, and repetitive traumatic exposures. Dissociative identity disorder represents another limit for us, like borderline personality disorder, in terms of whom we believe we can safely treat within the time frame used in our current work. We in fact do exclude people from treatment with this extreme dissociative disorder, again pointing to our treatment of adult survivors of incest who are likely in the *midrange of severity* in terms of the impact of the traumatic exposure.

Our idea of an adaptational blueprint derives from the work of Ronald Batson with people suffering from dissociative symptoms, including people in the most severe range. Before introducing this notion, there are several important assumptions we make about which there is a reasonable consensus among experts. First, dissociation is viewed as an *adaptation* to trauma, that is, a reasonable way of coping with intolerable circumstances at the time of their occurrence (see also Herman, 1992; Rieker & Carmen, 1986). Second, traumatic experiences often appear to get fixed in the mind as isolated fragments, often consisting of sensory perceptions or affective states, unassimilated and unaltered by the passage of time or subsequent experience (see especially van der Kolk & Fisler, 1995). Paradoxically, amnesia for some or all aspects of traumatic exposure is often accompanied by behavior that suggests the overwhelming presence or influence of a "memory." As Kardiner (1941, as referenced in van der Kolk & Fisler, 1995; van der Kolk et al., 1996) noted in describing war neurosis, suffering patients often developed amnesia for the trauma, while continuing to behave as if they were still in the middle of it. Current conceptualizations of traumatic memory are consistent with the idea that knowledge of traumatic material may be more readily accessible in the experiential system. They are also consistent with the widely observed phenomenon in adult survivors of incest of their "knowing" that they have been sexually abused in childhood without being able to give a coherent narrative of their experiences. Finally, the third related assumption in our work we wish to emphasize is that it is possible for survivors to achieve a state of mind in the course of psychotherapy that contextualizes previously unassimilated traumatic material and opens it to the influence of the therapeutic process and other positive life experiences (see also Horowitz, 1979; Roth & Batson, 1993).

In our discussion of the adaptational blueprint, dissociation is presented, after Batson (1992, 1994), as a mental operation based on the mind's ability to create states of consciousness that alternatively define reality, creating an imaginative illusion that becomes an important part of the trauma memory. Whereas the traumatic experience propels the creation of alternative states of consciousness, it precludes the natural capacities of relaxed absorption. The evolution of a reflective state of mind during psychotherapy counters trauma-driven experience, leading to a present-oriented experience of mastery and authentication.

TRAUMA MEMORY. In the case of incest, dissociation is an adaptation to the exposure to repeated abuse and represents attempts of the child to *redefine* the profound experiences that preempt her rights and individuality. Imaginative illusions that deny one's powerlessness create a survival logic that is like an adaptational blueprint, an evocative reproduction of the psychological plans constructed to cope with an intolerable situation or event. While intolerable formative events are not likely forgotten, they often seem to be transformed by the survival logic, which is an important part of the trauma memory and likely to be more readily accessible. The logic generates a symbolic language that describes the subjective reality of abuse, which in turn provides the basis for therapeutic dialogue.

The trauma memory often exists, then, not as a historical narrative but as states of mind, each with a "logical" point of view and with a persistent presence in the here and now. On the one hand, there are the remnants of the intolerable experiences in the form of revivifications, such as flashbacks or behavioral reenactments. On the other hand, there is the adaptational blueprint. In both cases the trauma is showing itself to be alive and well, as if one were still living in the past, in a state of terror or terror transformation. The memory is before us, frozen in time, defying attempts at exposure and forcing us to look in unconventional ways for what is right in front of our eyes.

REFLECTIVE APPRAISAL. The consideration of traumatic experiences is not possible if one is in a state of mind of terror or of defense against terror. A state of mind that is firmly grounded in the present and allows the person to stand back and dispassionately observe the past, while at the same time being acutely aware of the intense and overwhelming nature of emotion and meaning connected to the past, is what we mean by a reflective state of mind. It is like being in a state of dual consciousness, where one can both experience and see from the outside, if only in some small way, what one has worked so hard to transform, as it existed in the past.

The evolution of a reflective state of mind toward traumatic material during psychotherapy involves empathic and respectful consideration of the survival logic by both patient and therapist. The creation of a sense of pride in imaginatively surviving provides an appropriate perch from which to view the available data for piecing together something that approximates a narrative account. As patient and therapist observe the imprint of trauma in the broadest sense, witnessing the compelling complexity of newly coalescing information, the survivor can come to her own authenticated impression of her history with a sense of mastery over formerly disavowed experiences and the sense of mourning of an illusion.

CASE ILLUSTRATION: CECI. A review of videotaped sessions of individual therapy of one of our study participants, whom we will call Ceci, provided the data for the following illustration of the importance of focusing treatment on the adaptational blueprint. We observed tapes for 12 sessions of treatment, during which time the persistent presence of the trauma memory was readily apparent. A more detailed description of the following case material can be found in Batson (1994), and excerpts from actual therapy sessions during this period appear in chapter 5. Ceci had presented herself for treatment with the periodic intuition that she had been sexually abused as a child, an idea that she at other times doubted and hated herself for considering. Large gaps in her memory of her childhood were reported.

In the fourth session of individual therapy, Ceci reported having experienced a flashback to age 7 or 8 during a group therapy session the previous week. She felt as if she were in her grandfather's house during her annual winter stay, and she experienced, in a revivified form, "a dark, quiet isolation," with a sense of a presence at her bedroom door. The day following the flashback, she had an inexplicable reaction of feeling entrapped during sexual activity with her caring boyfriend.

To help Ceci deal with revivified material, she was first helped to relax into an absorbed state of mind while focusing on a peaceful image of her choosing. She envisioned a protected sunlit apartment of her own, which she shared with a vigilant dog, an image that evoked a sense of comfort in "owning her own space and being herself." This exercise in positive absorption emphasized that, in approaching revivified material, present-day well-being and control were a priority. While historical exploration was not to be avoided, it was made clear that it would be paced according to her ability to distinguish what held true for the present from what intruded from the past.

Over the next several sessions, Ceci adopted an imaginative metaphoric language that distinguished past from present and created a shared understanding of a prior adaptation that had kept her from important truths. As early as Session 5, she was able to observe a critical, mocking voice within herself that chastised her for ever considering that there could be safety. Her experience of danger in enjoyment or lowered vigilance, enjoyment of the kind associated with her sunlit apartment, was recognized as reminiscent of a time when constant vigilance may have been essential. This critical voice, mocking her also for being crazy to think something abusive had occurred, kept her from the fear associated with knowing. In Session 6, with encouragement to engage her imagination freely, Ceci reflected on a strong tactile awareness of wearing a burdensome shroud, a mask she was obliged to wear, that left her feeling inauthentic. The obligation felt as if she had made a deal that she did not remember. She experienced a realization that to be aware was to stop pretending. Relinquishing the shroud, she had a powerful sense of having found her "honest" voice. In the following session, although having vacillated between shrouded and more authentic viewpoints, Ceci felt a greater freedom to reappraise previously described aspects of her grandfather's house. As she reflected, she revived a detailed sense of being a 4- or 5-year-old child suspended in fear in the attic.

In Session 8, Ceci reported a dream about a black faceless man, the second dream she had had about him since the onset of therapy. She realized that he was not threatening but was rather linked to "a forgotten, protective element" within herself. During that week, she reported having awakened in a state of terror, gagging. The intensity of her awakening left her less doubtful about having known terror. In a reflective absorption, she described her comforting room. There was a darkness outside pressing in. The locked door was strained, but she realized that "it is going to hold." She heard the black figure, "challenging but not threatening," say, "I'm here behind you. I won't let you forget anymore." She reported her honest voice proclaiming, "I have nothing to lose to remember. It has already happened. I know I have survived." In Session 9 she reflected about the black figure. She heard him say, "Embrace the darkness." She assumed this meant that "it is better to know," recognizing the figure as a metaphoric characterization of prior amnesia. For her to understand the meaning and function of the black faceless man left her more convinced that "at the core" she is OK, not "a lunatic." Her developing confidence paralleled a broadening capacity for absorbed reflection. Ceci realized that the initial construction of her imagined safety, the sunlit apartment, bespoke a proximity to danger. She originally thought that the triangular shape of her apartment was a playful element, but she now understood that she felt safe only in the angle farthest from the door. She then had a dramatic, sudden revelation: the attic in her grandfather's house, the space where she was suspended in fear, was also triangular.

For Ceci, it was now possible to feel safe without having to obliterate any knowledge of danger. And it was possible to fathom a safety unencumbered by the burden of transforming a danger that no longer existed in her present day. By the end of the 3-month point, Ceci was comfortably engaged in the therapeutic process. With growing suspicions of her grandfather's betrayal, and confidence in her ability to find traces of her past in her evolving intuitive language, she approached the trauma memory as a competent scientist. More compelling to her than the *idea* of sexual abuse was the growing evidence of its imprint.

## Ceci and Miles

To aid in the understanding of the kinds of issues of identity and relationship facing adult survivors of childhood incest, we first present a group of poems written by Ceci that were presented to us at the end of her treatment. The poems were contained in a book entitled *Naming the Shadows, 1993–1994,* which had what looked like a picture of "the faceless man" on the front. We take these poems as expressions of Ceci's growing understanding of the legacy of what she experienced as a child.

Following Ceci's poems, we briefly describe the character and story of Miles, from Benjamin Britten's *The Turn of the Screw,* an opera adapted from a novella of the same name by Henry James. While the novella was written in 1898, the opera (with a libretto by Myfanwy Piper) was first performed in 1954. It is, of course, always humbling to find in literature or the arts a representation of something we as social scientists are studying that more poignantly captures the heart and soul of what we are trying to understand. Miles focuses us on the experience of a *child,* lest we forget that our concern is with women who were sexually abused as children. The symbolism of perpetrators as ghosts, and the failed attempts on the part of a caring governess to help Miles, are compelling aspects of the piece that we would like our readers to hold in mind. The experiences of both Ceci and Miles, when presented in this way, leave us with a more honest respect for the challenge we face as therapists.

*Stay*

I am here
and though the darkness
seeps in through my skin
and drowns the warmth
I've learned to save in store
I intend to stay.

*Naming the Shadows*

I am here
and even if my anger turns to fear and then
to love until I can't tell
when to close the door
I intend to stay.

I am here
and until the last ghost
leaves my soul and I have
all the laughter
I have ever wished and more
I intend to stay.


*fake*

"why can't you just fake it?"
that is a question you actually asked me.
please tell me you don't really need an answer.
please tell me that if you found me,
broken,
near death on the sidewalk,
that you would not make me get up and pretend I was ok,

you don't hate me because i'm not perfect.
that would require just a slight adjustment in tone,
a little spin, and the world would never know the difference.
slap a smile on, comb your hair,
do not let it show.

you hate me because I won't say I am perfect, won't say you are perfect.
I admitted a wound and you don't want it healed, you want it denied.
if I admit this wound then everyone will know that you've been
bleeding,

*Special Considerations in Treating Incest Survivors*

*bleeding,*
all over the spotless white carpet of our family name.
and you can have all the pain you can bear,
but you cannot make a mess.

"why can't you just fake it?"
please don't make me answer that.
if you truly ask that question in seriousness,
I will not try to hold back the anger that comes from a dirty child
trying not to leave a mark
in your sterile world.

you love me, though.
you love me for the promise
of being the perfect woman, the one to keep the house,
carry on the family lore
and tell it around the fire to my own terrified children.
you love what I could be,
if only I would see things your way.

but you can never be comfortable in my home.
the ragged edges of my lifestyle,
the naked decoration,
the joy and the trials I have painted on my walls,
carved into my furniture,
will not allow you to sit in ease.

"why can't you just fake it?"
I laughed when I first heard this question.
you couldn't even ask me directly, you had to ask someone else,
someone whose own answer would have melted your phone,
had you chosen to listen.

you have a right to be angry. you have worked so hard,

*Naming the Shadows*

*so hard*
to wrap your world in plastic
a hermetically sealed vacation
where you don't have to talk to the natives
or be bothered by unattractive people begging in the streets.
your closets are clean, your attic is dusted,
who am I to track mud
all over your beautiful house?

you have a right to be angry, but you don't know it.
you have a right to know that the dirt has been there all my life,
all your life,
and you will never rid yourself of it no matter how many times
you say you have no idea what I am talking about.
that damn spot will never leave until we put it on
and say we love wearing polka dots.

"why can't you just fake it?"
that's the best question you have asked me
since
"why can't you be normal?"


*Damn*

Your God and my God are different.

Your God spits gold, counts heads, keeps tabs

while my God sits and worries.

Your God justifies your wrath,
enables your rages,
cleans up your messes.
A wife in flowing robes,
a mother with a white beard,

an ever-indulging, never-questioning Santa Claus.
Everything you ever wanted for free, and you are
always right

My God holds my hand while I walk away.

My God keeps me from killing you.


*Naming the Shadows*

An ancestry of circled sisters,
naming the shadows
that sit at our shoulders, and breathe in our hair.
Call them forward to the center,
Become the light that will consume them.
Celebrate their death, consecrate this time.

Huddle around the fire of Truth,
know that some would have *us* burned, as well.
Heretics, Witches, Liars.
History will always find a name for smaller
truth-tellers,
and stakes will always be the measure of
the status quo,
not the bottom line.

So our effigies may light up family dinners
and these shadows may live well in other
nightmare halls.
But our souls are bright with fire
Our memories have burned a path beyond this sky
and Time will always justify the healer
and feed the hunger
of the victim of the crime.

If you read the poems carefully, you will begin to understand that it really is a matter of life or death. That to know oneself in laughter and love and truth is to have a *vital* core, sustaining life. That the suffering imposed by the annihilation of will inherent in the abuse of children by family members and other caretakers is lethal. That the heart remembers, and to keep the heart alive is often too painful. That one can survive such profound alienation from one's family only by finding one's self in relationship to trust-worthy others.

## The Turn of the Screw

During the first act of the opera, we learn something about Miles's relationship to the ghost of Quint, his abuser and former caretaker, and about the way his current governess struggles to understand how she can help this child whom she both loves and fears. She fears him because of what she must face in trying to help him: the knowledge of the corruption of innocence. She fears him, too, be-cause he seems to embody, at times, the very evil perpetrated against him.

Miles is portrayed as a beautiful, talented, brilliant, and charming child, whose behavior, at times, unpredictably seems to mimic that of Quint's, in both its sexualized qualities and its sadistic ones. We see how Quint has seduced him by cleverly creating a special status for Miles in the context of Miles's dependence on him. When Quint is present, as a ghost, Miles is indeed allied with him, loyal, almost mesmerized, and Miles faithfully keeps the secret of their relation-ship, out of confusion about what is in his best interests. We see clearly, in watching Quint and Miles relate, how sensible it is for Miles to incorporate the point of view that Quint so effectively holds Miles captive with: that their relationship is something that

Miles should cherish. We see, too, that whether or not he maintains this illusion, he is helpless in the face of Quint's power. In Quint's words:

> I seek a friend
> Obedient to follow where I lead
> Slick as a juggler's mate
> To catch my thought
> Proud, curious, agile
> He shall feed my mounting power
> Then to his bright subservience
> I'll expound
> The desperate passions of a haunted heart
> And in that hour
> The ceremony of innocence is drowned

The last line here is actually taken from a poem written by W.B. Yeats, "The Second Coming," which was first published in 1921. The first six lines of the poem call forward the idea of a turning screw, a bird of prey, that destroys the very core, or center, or soul of a young child:

> Turning and turning in the widening gyre
> The falcon cannot hear the falconer;
> Things fall apart; the centre cannot hold;
> Mere anarchy is loosed upon the world,
> The blood-dimmed tide is loosed, and everywhere
> The ceremony of innocence is drowned

At first when the governess discovers that there is a ghost who is endangering Miles, she wants to protect him by keeping him from seeing or knowing this ghost of Quint, who she understands was depraved and had in some way hurt Miles. As she realizes that Quint continues to control Miles through his ghost, she is initially overwhelmed by the gravity of the situation and her sense of powerlessness to provide help.

In the second act of the opera, we see more clearly how Miles is suffering and how at times he is tempted, with his growing trust of the governess, to expose Quint and open up to her that part of himself that knows Quint is evil. It is perhaps only in the context of his relationship with the governess that Miles can in fact see clearly what Quint has done. Fearing that Miles will be destroyed by the ghost of Quint and responding to challenges by Miles to act on his behalf, the governess is determined to help Miles break the secret bond with Quint and to destroy Quint's enduring control.

In the last scene of the opera, Miles is staged between the governess and Quint, as the governess pleads with Miles to tell her about Quint, and Quint insists that Miles not betray their secret. It is as if Miles is being torn apart, and in fact this is one explanation for Miles's death upon naming Quint's ghost. As the ghost is destroyed, so is Miles.

This is a sobering opera. Ghosts, as a haunting memory, are not so easy to see, even when we care to look for them. And they are even harder to put in their place.


## Conclusions

We have attempted to establish, in this chapter, an understanding of the kinds of problematic issues of identity and relationship facing adult survivors of childhood incest. The targets of treatment we described, namely complex posttraumatic stress disorder, trauma themes, and the adaptational blueprint, add a broader focus to the treatment of posttraumatic stress disorder symptoms. They are consistent with the conceptualization of incest as a traumatic set of experiences that require an extraordinary adaptation to intolerable conditions of family life for the child. This adaptation to traumatic life circumstances disrupts normative processes relating to self and social development. The wide array of symptoms associated with childhood sexual abuse, including dissociative symptoms, must be understood in relationship to a traumatic adaptation. Considering a particular set of symptoms in isolation, without concern for this bigger picture, can be fraught with difficulty. Empathic failures can result from maintaining a decontextualization of the sexual abuse.

Our targets of treatment represent our consideration of a number of different scholarly threads in the study of trauma, all of which insist on a more complex representation of the impact of incest than is captured by simple PTSD. Complex PTSD represents a constellation of trauma symptoms, consistently observed by clinician-scholars, that are associated with PTSD, and they extend a continuum of severity within the traditional diagnostic nomenclature. Trauma themes represent the subjective construction of meaning given to traumatic experience and are one way to understand how the adaptation to traumatic experience continues to drive experience in the present day. Work relating to the definition and measurement of themes derives from traditions in the social sciences that underscore the value of the subject's own voice as well as the complexity of subjective experience and its construction in representations of the self in relation to others. The focus on an adaptational blueprint acknowledges the trauma-transforming nature of one's adaptation to childhood sexual abuse within the family and illustrates how the transforming blueprint can often provide the key to opening unassimilated traumatic material to the influence of the therapeutic process. This work derives from a tradition of clinical discourse in the field of dissociation and takes us closer still to the inner world of our subjects.

Finally, we have tried to convey our commitment to contextualizing our systematic work in a fuller, more intuitive understanding of the complexity of the experience of a child who has suffered intolerable exploitation, and of its enduring presence into adulthood. Only with this kind of understanding can we hope to achieve the necessary respect for the challenge involved in our therapeutic work.

*Chapter 2*

# Individual and Group Psychotherapy for Incest Survivors

T his chapter provides an overview of our work in the contexts of individual and group psychotherapy. While we will provide illustrative case material here and throughout the book, it is not our intention to dictate specific procedures for therapists to follow, but rather to make our therapeutic assumptions and goals clear so they may serve as a guide to others in their work. We maintain throughout that the provision of a therapeutic context involves creativity in the level and timing of communications in order for therapeutic messages to be comprehended both rationally and experientially. Although we are clear in what we are trying to accomplish in the therapy, when teaching our students we leave room for their own individual styles to mold the actual therapeutic dialogue. It is less important to us, for example, *how* a therapist conveys her or his trustworthiness and integrity as a person and as a therapist than *that* she or he conveys it in a compelling way.

The heart of this chapter is a description of what is involved in establishing a therapeutic social context. We believe that the overriding goal of psychotherapy is to establish a *context* in which the survivor can begin to tolerate the emotional intensity and meaning initially attached to the sexual abuse, and in which a thoughtful, reflective construction of information can develop. In explaining what we mean by social context in the first section of this chapter, we introduce our study participant Jesse, and a character from musical theater, Mary Lennox. In our description of the therapeutic social context in the second section, we introduce a survivor whom we call Samantha. We close with case illustrations, in the individual and group psychotherapy domains, from our study subjects Annie and Jo.

## Reflective Construction in a Social Context

As Judith Herman (1992) poignantly describes, the extraordinary adaptation required by a child to cope with repeated sexual violation by a trusted family member occurs in a context where other adults who are responsible for her care do not protect her. This lack of protection, regardless of how it comes about or how it manifests itself, makes it even more formidable for the abused child to preserve any sense of herself as a worthy, agentic person living in a benign social world. This lack of protection defines a social context that is in sharp contrast to one where help is provided to allow a child to understand an abusive experience for what it is, and to grieve in the warmth of someone else's understanding, perspective, compassion, and strength.

A thoughtful, reflective reconstruction of trauma-related information by an adult survivor allows for the incorporation of traumatic experience into a coherent belief structure that is more adaptive and mindful of other points of view than the one dictated by the abuse and all its supporting surround. Even when a coherent narrative for what happened is not established, the reflective appraisal of states of mind relating to the traumatic experience provides an important experience of mastery and authentication, which powerfully counters trauma-driven experience. But standing back to bring something like this into focus requires help, now as well as then, partly because of the social nature of identity. It is this point about our therapy that we are going to lay the groundwork for here, starting with an elaboration of what we asserted in chapter 1 about the kinds of data survivors have to work with in locating the truth about their past.

## The Therapeutic Data

The most profound psychological scholarship seems to be that which orients us to the most basic human truths and points of human connection. By basic human truths we mean those human qualities that are the bedrock of our social selves and that connect us by virtue of our common ground. As human beings, we all understand these truths at some level of our experience, and it is incumbent on those of us who are social scientists to stand back in order to bring into focus what is already commonly understood, ever-present, and in some way, overlooked. So, for example, while no one would argue against the fundamental value of physical contact or comfort provided by another person, particularly at moments of distress, this is certainly not a self-consciously celebrated fact of social life. In fact, as late as the 1950s, social scientists were still debating the existence of a primary need for physical closeness, and we can credit Harry Harlow, a distinguished psychologist, for setting us straight, so to speak, on this matter.

Similarly, survivors have to stand back in order to bring into focus the ever-present but overlooked trauma memory that is so self-defining and that exists in the revivifications and adaptational transformations of the abusive experience. These revivifications and transformations are the data that are so compelling to survivors who have typically been struggling for a long time to understand what was wrong with them because of their symptoms, or failed relationships, or blocked potential, or sense of alienation from themselves and others. They have been trying to understand what is wrong with them, but they have been looking in the wrong place.

One of the things that makes these two kinds of observable data—the revivifications and the adaptational blueprint—so persuasive, in addition to how each uniquely shows the trauma to be alive, is their relationship to each other: two truths that are opposites, and yet the same. So survivors can have the experience of feeling both terrified and not afraid at all; that someone means everything to them one moment and nothing at all the next; that the therapy is stupid because nothing happened to them and because it is too painful to look at what did happen. It is compelling for survivors to realize that they wouldn't be counterphobic if they weren't afraid, or be vigilant if they felt safe, or idealize people if they believed others' shortcomings were tolerable.

The observable data, as clarifying as they are once they are seen, are not so easy to bring into focus, however. Revivifications, in the form of flashbacks and behavioral reenactments, are not always easy to recognize as such. Flashbacks can broadly be considered to include, for example, moments of feeling ashamed as they did when their mother acted dismissive or contemptuous toward them as a child when they asked for help. And adaptations that transformed intolerable experiences are even harder to recognize as such. When Miles acted like Quint, it was like a rationalization of Quint's behavior—making something revered out of something corrupt. He wouldn't have wanted to be like him if he saw Quint's behavior for what it was.

One of the things that is essential as a survivor for seeing your self [*sic*] in this way, is to be able to, in effect, look into the eyes of someone else to see what they see. In saying this, we are making some assumptions about the social nature of identity that lay the foundation for our ideas about what is involved in establishing a therapeutic social context that allows survivors to do the trauma work.

## Social Context

Charles Cooley (1902), a scholar still highly influential today among social psychologists and sociologists, was brilliant in his reliance on the naive meaning of *self*. When putting forward his ideas about the social construction of self, he defines human nature as fundamentally social. Cooley describes self as a "feeling of self" that is instinctive and that develops through experience in the social world. It is like a readiness that presumes a social reference, often in the form of a reflected or looking-glass self. He writes about "living in the minds of others," not in any self-conscious way, but in a way that is just as fundamental as walking on solid ground, "without thinking how it bears us up." He notes how coldness and contempt from others leads to the sense of being outcast and helpless. Here again is the idea that to sustain a sense of oneself as a worthy, agentic person requires the kind of social interchange that reflects that experience loud and clear.

Lack of protection defines a social context that sustains a lie, in some form, about the nature of what is or has been going on that is abusive. It sustains a point of view about what has happened, or is happening, that would be inconsistent with the point of view of a compassionate outsider. We are reminded of a play produced recently at the Workhouse Theater in New York City called *In Ten Cities* that illustrates this point beautifully. Myra and her husband, Tom, have just been informed by Social Services that their child is showing all the signs of having been sexually abused, as reported by the child's school, and that the family is going to be evaluated by them. We, as an audience, then get an opportunity to observe Myra and Tom spending time together in the face of this accusation. All of their behavior is consistent with the makings of a home without protection for a child, and this point of view is clearly held by the audience. For Myra and Tom, however, the reality is portrayed as being quite different. In the midst of Tom's drunken railings at Social Services, and Myra's absorption in TV, we see them allied in their mutual reassurances that "there is nothing wrong here."

It is not just any point of view from a compassionate outsider that will do, however. We are talking about the provision of a social context where the self that was lost in the confusion of surviving gets reflected and an honest presentation of self becomes possible. It is similar to a point made in a contemporary scholarly study of *self* in which Scheibe (1995) tells about a gay man who has finally come out of the closet. He writes, "The camouflage was finally shucked off with the splendid discovery that the world around him had become sufficiently tolerant to make an honest presentation of self sustainable" (p. 3).

We as therapists cannot change the fact of what happened to a survivor at the hands of her abuser or abusers. We can, however, provide a context different from what was provided then, a context in which we help someone to hold on to herself. It is like helping someone locate a capacity, or a potential, rather than creating something that wasn't previously there. To say that a survivor has been alienated from herself is not very different, really, from saying that she has been alienated from any reasonable social context. We think Ceci is talking about persisting at finding a life-sustaining social intimacy and sense of self when in her poems she alludes to circled sisters huddled around the fire of truth, and when she says that she will stay until the last ghost leaves her soul and she has all the laughter she could have ever wished and more.

We will build on this fundamental notion of social context as we describe the *therapeutic* social context that provides the help people need to process the therapeutic data before them. First, to solidify our groundwork here, we would like to create two contrasting images of caretakers responding to children in the aftermath of trauma: the mother of Jesse, one of our study subjects, and the maid to Mary Lennox from *The Secret Garden.*

## Jesse and Mary Lennox

Jesse's parents' behavior effectively negated her as a person. They were trying to mold her into what they wanted her to be, apparently at all costs. Self-assertion was considered disloyal and was punished with beatings by her father that were often incited by her mother's ridicule of and disdain for Jesse. Sexual abuse by her father represented more of the same to Jesse, a way to control her, while bolstering his sense of power and esteem. She kept herself concealed. She faked it to survive.

While Jesse had always had a clear memory of the repeated sexual abuse by her father from age 12 until she left for college, she had denied its effects in order to stay connected to her family. She spoke to her parents about the sexual abuse for the first time approximately a year after her graduation from college. Even though her father superficially admitted to what he had done, her mother appeared more angry about the upheaval in the family caused by Jesse's disclosure than by the destructiveness of her husband's actions. She was dismissive of the abuse, complaining that Jesse was making a mountain out of a molehill. Her mother could not forgive her for disclosing this secret. For Jesse, her mother's response was as unforgivable to her as her father's betrayal. Jesse's mother continued to be supportive of Jesse's father throughout various confrontations in the course of the therapy.

Not surprisingly, it was hard for Jesse to trust her own point of view about things, and she often took her estranged husband's accusations to heart. In arguments with her husband, some of what she had kept hidden about her feelings toward her father and mother came alive in response to her husband's supercilious behavior. She said that arguments would begin with her being angry and confrontational and would gradually give way, in response to her husband's harshly stated difference of opinion, to a doubting of the validity of her opinions, and then to an experience of helpless confusion reminiscent of experiences from her childhood.

Jesse's internalization of her mother's and father's contempt for her point of view, for her very being, led to her alienation from others in another way. It was hard for her to experience common ground with others even in a reasonable social context, like the psychotherapy group. It was hard not to focus on points of differences that were not, in reality, irreconcilable. The contempt that she felt from her parents had made her feel like an outcast, while at the same time requiring that she set herself apart if she were to hold on to the truth.

Jesse felt helpless about setting the record straight in her family of origin, where she still longed to find a sense of community. She continued throughout therapy, without success, to try to open her mother's mind to her point of view about what had gone on in the family. She regretted every time that she confided in her mother. While her paternal grandmother, whom she had lived with for some time as a small child, had provided a loving environment she cherished in her memory, Jesse perceived her as loving her son, Jesse's father, in a way that precluded her setting the record straight there as well.

The psychological horror of being trapped in this morass of twisted loyalties, as a context for coming to terms with a profound betrayal being masqueraded as fatherly love, is obvious. In contrast to this is the simplicity one can imagine in providing a psychological anchor that allows someone the possibility of enduring the loss. In

*The Secret Garden,* a musical written by Marsha Norman based on the novel of the same name by Frances Hodgson Burnett, Mary Lennox is a young girl who has lost everyone she has known and loved to cholera. The maid where she is staying, Martha, in her intuitive wisdom, is able to comfort Mary, who relives the epidemic in her nightmares and is feeling deeply lost. She sings to Mary in a song entitled "Hold On":

What you've got to do is
Finish what you have begun
I don't know just how
But it's not over 'till you've won

When you see the storm is comin'
See the lightning part the skies
It's too late to run
There's terror in your eyes
What you do then is remember
This old thing you heard me say
It's the storm, not you
That's bound to blow away

Hold on
Hold on to someone standin' by
Hold on
Don't even ask how long or why
Child, hold on to what you know is true
Hold on 'til you get through
Child, oh child
Hold on

When you feel your heart is poundin'
Fear the devil's at your door

There's no place to hide
You're frozen to the floor
What you do then is you force yourself
To wake up and you say
It's the dream not me
That's bound to go away


## The Therapeutic Social Context

We are trying to help survivors hold on to themselves with life-sustaining social intimacy while they assess with a new clarity how they have been affected by what happened to them as a child. As a survivor is *permitted*, perhaps for the first time, to recognize and accept the intensity of painful feelings and self-defining constructs associated with the sexual abuse and her family's response to it, and as she is permitted to respectfully regard the ways she has coped with what happened, trauma-driven experience becomes open to the influence of the therapeutic process and to other positive life experiences. The therapeutic process challenges and limits the power of the family abuse and neglect to overwhelm representations of the self, others, and the world more generally. The measurement of trauma themes over the course of therapy reflects the evolving newly contextualized meaning assigned to traumatic life experience.

The individual and group therapies are mutually reinforcing in the creation of a context that helps the survivor locate self. A secure, encompassing self emerges in the contexts of an intimate relationship with an authority in individual therapy on the one hand, and a group of compassionate peers (authorized by a second "expert") in group therapy on the other. While one-on-one work goes on in the group as well as the individual therapy context, often by way of solidifying individual therapy accomplishments, it has the special characteristic of also harnessing the broader group consensus and connection in bringing to light hidden meanings and feelings related to common abusive experiences. In the privacy of the individual therapy, the more intense alliance with the therapist firmly establishes a balance between autonomy and protection as well as a method of creative scientific detective work.

In *The Turn of the Screw*, the well-meaning and caring governess is determined to have Miles tell her of the abuse he has endured. She is convinced that it is the only way to break the spell that the ghost of Quint seems to have cast on Miles. While there is wisdom in this plan, of course, to carry it through successfully is actually a delicate and complex matter. For one thing, Miles has been convinced by the malevolent Quint that secrecy is just a part of their special, intimate bond. Miles is driven both by loyalty to, and fear of, Quint's ghost in keeping silent. For another, he has a construction of the abuse that is consistent with what Quint has told him in order to hold him captive. For the most part, Miles is not aware that there is something happening to him that is annihilating. Finally, while he understands intuitively that the governess offers the kind of protection and love a *child* needs, and while he is drawn to her because of this, he relates to her in a pseudomature and sexualized way that hides his profound vulnerability. Although the governess holds the promise for Miles of seeing more clearly what Quint has done, her insistence that he *simply* tell her what has happened misses the essence of what binds him. As we move through a description of the therapeutic social context, we hope it will become clearer how challenging the provision of therapeutic communication can be.

A focus on the process of *communication* as an important agent of change has a distinguished intellectual history. The writing of Jurgen Ruesch, for example, an influential figure in interpersonal psychiatry, establishes therapeutic communication as an activity as old as human language and as broadly conceived as a basic tenet of social influence. Interestingly, he notes that traumatic memories can be detraumatized when they are elaborated under the right conditions of interpersonal feedback (Ruesch, 1966). With the appropriate communication, he argues, a therapist can lead somebody to "show" themselves, or open themselves to therapeutic influence. In this vein, we maintain that "appropriate" communications often require messages that are comprehended both rationally *and* experientially, since aspects of the traumatic reality are discoverable only in fantasy or on the level of feeling, that is, at the experiential level. Creative communications often provide the means needed to get people to pay attention to themselves—to validate affect, for example, that is inconsistent with the disconfirming logic adopted from the perpetrator or others in the family. We are reminded of an example from a therapy group where one member raised a question, quite seriously at first, of whether she could be prosecuted for murder if she were to dig up and shoot her dead father. The question and playful but respectful response from the therapist lead to humorous discussion in which all group members participated and which centered around how to creatively dig up dead perpetrators. It was a context in which it was OK to be murderous, and it brought rage to a realm where it could live without shame. It was both patently absurd and marvelously evocative, a pleasurably intimate experience that made the emotional intensity of helpless rage tolerable.

It is worth rereading Ceci's poems presented in chapter 1 at this point. She tells us about laughter and rage and intimacy and truth, and about how she has been affected by what happened to her as a child. We believe that what allowed her to safely tell us about herself involved three provisions of our social context: *autonomy, protection,* and *playfulness.*

### Allowing Autonomy and Agency

Jesse had to hold a part of herself back in order not to be completely annihilated by the sexual abuse at the hands of her father, as well as by the generally contemptuous and dismissive way in which both her parents related to her. There was pressure in her family against her being fully present. To dismiss is to show indifference or disregard, refusing to accept or recognize. To be contemptuous is to belittle, despise, and disgrace. Disregarding or regarding with disdain are the opposite of what we need to do as therapists. Our task is to authorize adult survivors of childhood incest to experience greater clarity about what happened to them and how it has affected their lives.

In relationships in general, to *recognize* others means that they have to be seen as something more than an extension of your needs. They cannot experience or grow into who they are if you are defining it for them, by an assertion of who *you* are, or who *you* would like them to be, even if that someone is a child. In the case of sexual abuse, if you put *your* sexuality in someone else's face, so to speak, they will never discover their own. Even the relatively benign insistence on the governess's part that Miles name his abuser was an insistence born of her own insecurity about what was going on and her need to make it better. Paradoxically, one of the things you must offer someone else if you want them to show themselves to you is privacy. This means that the typical expectation in therapy that the more disclosure the better is held up for scrutiny here. We are reminded of an extreme instance of the need for privacy in a client who used to read her poems to us, which quite explicitly spoke of her father's sexual abuse of her, but she would never admit, if asked, to any knowledge of her father's exploitation.

To regard survivors with respect in contrast to disdain necessarily requires that the therapist adopt, and communicate to the survivor, the notion that she is a worthy, agentic person. The therapist should assume that the survivor is the expert about her experiences, and that this expertise will define the boundaries of what will be accepted, or not accepted, in terms of outside constructions. This includes a therapeutic attitude that conveys the message that the survivor should realize a sense of pride in having imaginatively survived childhood abuse. If your child, or someone else's, is pushed off their bike by some bully and comes around looking for comfort from you, you don't ask them why the bully picked on *them* or why they've never learned to ride a bike better. You ask what happened, so that they can express themselves, and then you go from there to support their competencies in coming to terms with an imperfect world.

We have previously written about Samantha, an incest survivor we treated, in an article, "The Creative Balance" (Roth & Batson, 1993). The title referred to the challenge in providing a survivor with a sense of autonomy, or independence, while at the same time providing an essential social connection, or protection. Whereas contempt leads to a sense of being outcast and helpless, the therapeutic context leads to a sense of connection and agency. To convey from a survivor's perspective what we have tried to describe about the provision of a sense of autonomy or agency, we include the following poem written by Samantha to the second author (RB) in the course of therapy. By way of brief background, RB had covered her with a blanket in response to her saying she felt exposed while recounting, with her eyes closed, some of what had happened to her as a child. She routinely used the blanket for privacy, and it had become a symbol of what she got from the therapeutic relationship that she could literally hold on to as she moved through the trauma

*Individual and Group Psychotherapy for Incest Survivors*

work. This poem anticipates our discussion of protection and play-fulness and illustrates Samantha's new-found sense of identity.

(This *must* be read rhythmically.)

I don't want to mislead you
into thinking I need you
or that you're the only one
' Cause while it may sound queer
Ronald Batson dear
*It's the blanket that I love.*

Now don't misunderstand, you're a hell of a guy
You're everything a person could want
You're gentle and kind with a creative mind
and quick and knowing and fun
So it may be hard to understand why
*It's the blanket I really love.*

Now this is not without it's problems, let me tell
you how:
The blanket belongs to you
And no doubt provides for others, a perfect aid
to the things you so intuitively do
Now it's not that I don't have blankets of my own
My mother even made me two (oh god!)
But yours has the magic of making me whole
Something no other blanket can do.

*It's the blanket I love,* trust me, *please*
I may have led you astray
I close my eyes and I feel my soul
I let myself go to heal my heart

I don't *need* you in any way
Except maybe a little to hear your voice, whatever
it is you say
Or to look in your eyes to see what you see
Or to know you know what's inside of me.

But it's the *blanket* that makes me warm and safe
and holds my fear and cries
And maybe when it's over I'll walk away
Like from an old friend saying good-bye
Or maybe you'll let me take it home.

## Providing Protection

For Samantha, the blanket provided a protective covering that sym-
bolized privacy, containment, safety, intimacy, comfort, and rest.
With this level of protection, the search for a deeper understanding
of what had transpired in her childhood was naturally self-enhancing. It provided for a stripping away of layers of confusion that had
resulted from a child's attempt to protect herself from an overwhelming reality, from perpetrators' power to define things in their
self-interest, and from other family members' need to dismiss or lay
blame. It allowed for an acknowledgment of intense feelings associated with the ugly truth of family betrayal, which then, like an aging
enemy or ghost that she could finally look in the eye, no longer controlled her. And no one would question whether the danger of the
enemy was equal to the intensity of the emotional reaction. It was
understood that a ghost can be powerful, unless one names it under
the right set of circumstances. The protection made it possible to
know that there was somebody to lean on that was worthy of trust.
In Samantha's own words, writing in the third person, she describes
her early work in an absorbed state of mind:

She was grateful for the lack of suspiciousness,
the warmth, the decisiveness
She could sink into the couch and turn inward to
the sound of almost musically timed counts
The sense of someone else gently and sensitively in charge
He offered her the blanket as a way of helping her
to be more private and more contained
He placed it on her like an adult would a child,
to provide comfort in sleep or rest
She was safe at last to go back and uncover those
frozen memories that so cruelly provided the
driving force in so many aspects of her some 30 odd
years of life.

The use of the blanket as a signal of protection evolved in the context of the relationship between Samantha and RB. It was initially a spontaneous response by RB to Samantha's anxiety about disclosure, and it remained an evocative way to communicate about different aspects of the provision of protection that would have been hard to put into words.

In approaching revivified material, it is crucial to remember that present-day well-being and control are a priority and that historical exploration will be paced according to the ability to distinguish what holds true in the present from what intrudes from the past. The therapeutic data, in the form of revivifications and adaptational transformations, have to be set apart, in effect, to be viewed from the outside with the intellectual curiosity of a scientist or a detective. "Standing back" brings with it perspective *and* safety. The survivor needs to be in *control* of the trauma memory, to have a secure expectation of controlled exposure, where affect can be modulated and where one gets to *choose* to experience what before was unbidden and overwhelming. And the survivor needs to be in control of communicating about the trauma memory in whatever way is comfortable. Survivors have to be able, for example, to "say it without saying it," and they have to be encouraged to be thoughtful about their experience of "knowing and not knowing," in contrast to being cornered into a state of certainty. The therapist is like a heart monitor that the survivor hooks up to, so that she can relax into a secured state of mind where she can, paradoxically, "let go" to do the trauma work.

A reflective state of mind counters states of mind that are either absorbed with terror or constricted and hypervigilant in defense against terror. These latter states of mind, which represent another way of thinking about the symptoms of posttraumatic stress disorder, disallow the thoughtful consideration of the trauma memory. An alternative kind of absorption must be created that is compelling enough to encourage a hopeful engagement of traumatic material. Locating this state of absorption involves giving one's mind free reign in the context of a secure attachment, and sharing meaningful and often playful interchanges. In the context of this trusting attachment that was not available in the abusive family, loss and deprivation become clearer, but not irreparable. All of what was chased away—the capacities for self-respect, loving attachments, and the experience of intensely absorbing *positive* affect—become reavailable, or reabsorbing, and the impact of trauma is confined. Only the compelling intensities of these capacities are a reparative match for the spell-like preoccupation with the terror and its reverberations.

The experience of absorption in being *yourself* in intimate relation to another person, then, creates a sense of security and pleasure and allows for a consideration of the trauma memory from firm ground. The use of humor and imagination, in addition to the provision of autonomy and protection, contextualize the traumatic material in this alternative absorption that would have been naturally accessible without the impact of trauma.

## Being Playful

The work of Emanuel Hammer (1990), provides a wonderful articulation of the use of imagery, metaphor, humor, and creativity as a means of connecting with other people's affect and helping them find a way to their feelings. He compares the usual therapeutic interpretive intervention with a poet's statement, noting that in the former, what is often missing is "the tonus necessary to carry the emotional reality that allows more full-bodied connection" (p. xv). He convincingly makes an argument for what, after the fact, seems almost obvious: that "the muscle and surprise of language" (p. 66) holds the power to help someone toward a better sense of her or himself, as well as toward a deeper sense of intimate contact with the other person. Sharing an imaginative or humorous interchange creates an intimate, playful ambiance that has a unique advantage in getting to the heart of things.

For both of us in our own way, the ability to establish an imaginative or humorous context in which to approach traumatic material is critical to what we do as therapists. While there is always an underlying sadness in the therapeutic work—about the pain in individuals' lives and about the failure of society when adults treat children in such an annihilating way—there is also an exhilaration in seeing people sharing in playful intimacy, even after all they have been through. It speaks to a kind of heroism on the part of survivors whom we have treated, that they remain hopeful about the possibility for self-knowledge and meaningful human exchange.

*Naming the Shadows*

If you were to watch a tape of the group sessions, you would be struck by the laughter that often fills the room, and in the individual sessions, by a warm playfulness between two people, created by using words and images from the survivor's language. The following imaginative piece written to RB by Samantha not only captures important qualities of the therapeutic context we have been trying to convey, but like Ceci's poems, illustrates the level of communication we strive to achieve:

*Well, you and I were on this island—sort of like Gilligan's Island—you know, that TV show with Dobey Gillis. Anyhow, we were gathering materials from the woods to weave into this kind of container—a basket, I guess—to hold some things we had been collecting that would ultimately serve us in our rescue off the island. We weren't talking much, and while our relationship to one another wasn't terribly well defined, we seemed comfortably enough engaged in this common purpose. It's funny, I remember thinking about how life has a certain harmony at times that makes you feel safe or optimistic or peaceful, or something like that. Well, you were picking these berries for some reason I didn't quite understand, but then I had gotten used to you doing some weird things from time to time. Turns out you had this idea that we could use them for a kind of glue that would prevent the basket from having spaces where things could fall through. Anyhow, when we'd done enough work for one day, we headed back to the place where all the others were gathered to get something prepared for dinner. We helped each other get these thorny things off our backs that had gotten stuck from the woods, and then I think you were going to help out with dinner, and I was going off to do something else. I remember thinking about how kind of odd it was that things were running so smoothly, given that we were all stranded on this island—almost suspended in time from any re-*

*ality—and yet in another way engaged in a very real and complex process of survival.*

## Summary

At this point, a more linear review of the important points made thus far is in order before we go on to illustrate them with case material. This listing of the major arguments should provide a helpful structure for taking in the clinical presentations.

1. The overriding goal of psychotherapy is to establish a context in which to daylight a survivor's experience of sexual abuse, an experience that typically is emotionally overwhelming and self-defining.

2. The perpetrator(s)' strong message, the family's lack of protection, and the child's survival logic or adaptational blueprint provide layers of distortion and confusion that make it difficult to recognize the impact of abuse.

3. Bringing the ever-present, overlooked trauma memory into focus requires reflective appraisal of revivification and adaptational transformation of the abusive experience. This is a self-enhancing process because it is authenticating and because it limits the power of the traumatic experience to be self-defining.

4. To help survivors present themselves with greater clarity about what happened to them and how it has affected their lives, the therapeutic context provides autonomy, protection, and playfulness, which lead to a sense of agency and connection.

5. The experience of absorption in being oneself in intimate relation to another person creates a sense of security and plea-

sure that allows for a reflective consideration of the trauma memory.

6. The provisions of the therapeutic context are often communicated on a number of different levels simultaneously, making contact with both rational and experiential systems.

## Annie

Annie never claimed, in the course of psychotherapy, to remember something she had not known before. She did, however, have a growing awareness of her inability to hold in mind, over the years, just how bad what had happened to her really was. She came to see her abuse of alcohol and drugs as a way of obliterating what were emotionally overwhelming reminders of a childhood filled with abuse and neglect. She remembered being drawn to sad, fearful, abandoned animals as a child, and recalled her own deep sense of aloneness and yearning for loving protection. She was apparently either left out on her own or targeted for physical and sexual abuse by family members, and there wasn't even anyone around to make her feel proud about how she survived. A person she remembers greatly admiring, a girlfriend of her older brother's, tragically killed herself when Annie was only 8 years old. Annie understood that extreme situations called for extreme responses.

In this family context, Annie seems to have found at least two ways to redefine her powerlessness and to cope with deprivation and harm. On the one hand, she tried to maintain the belief that if she loved the abusive men in her family enough, she would someday be deserving of their loving kindness in return. On the other hand, in contrast to this solution of finding power in choosing subordination, she found safety in dangerous places where others would not go. She remembered, in the 8th month of therapy, for example, on a trip back to her childhood home, that there was a high, narrow rim that she would walk on around the silo to a safe escape from her sadistic brother, who was too afraid to follow. It was like beating them at their own game, albeit at great danger to herself. In a similar attainment of power and freedom, she found great pleasure in riding her pony, unfortunately without an appreciation of the need for caution about harming herself.

The reality of Annie's childhood abuse was emotionally overwhelming and self-defining, both in the past and in the present. She continued, as an adult, to subordinate her needs to those of exploitative men, in two marriages, one in which her husband was extremely dangerous and violent. She also continued to endanger her life in her job as an ironworker in a hostile male culture by priding herself in walking on beams without fear or protective restraints. Continuing to feel dirty and unimportant, and expecting humiliation in response to her vulnerabilities and needs, riding motorcycles at 95 miles an hour was experienced as taking a strong stand. There was an integrity, also, in holding herself apart from others because she really didn't expect anybody to understand.

Annie thought that people who were privileged could not truly understand anything about deprivation of the kind she had experienced. We believe she nevertheless sought treatment in our study because she intuitively understood that there was a better way than she had come upon on her own to deal with the ever-present trauma memory. Annie was genuinely motivated to come to a greater clarity about how her childhood experience had affected her adult life. At the same time, she insisted that her life's work at adaptation be treated with respect, an insistence that at times was difficult to respond to empathically. It was this insistence, in part, that ultimately made the alliance with other group members too difficult for her. For example, at a group meeting when the first author (SR) was absent, and only her less experienced cotherapist was present, Annie began cleaning her finger nails with a large pocket knife, frightening and angering the other group members. This act of challenging the group members' ability to understand her need to be tough actually alienated her from her caring peers. Her alienation led to her leaving the group after 6 months of treatment.

We have discussed how a victim of incest will likely experience confusion surrounding her abuse, which is due to the perpetrator's distortion, the other family members' collusion or denial, and the child's own defensive survival logic. This confusion often manifests itself in a complexity to relationships that mirror earlier relationships in the sense that they were defined by such opposites as anger and shame, loyalty and betrayal, helplessness and resiliency, and so on. In Annie's case, even in regard to just this single incident in the group, we suspect her confusion about whether she or the others had done something wrong overwhelmed the possibility of sharing a meaningful connection with the group members. She must have been ashamed, for example, of causing others to be afraid of her anger, at the same time that she felt betrayed by their fear. In Annie's mind, the group members didn't seem to understand her need to establish the character of her resiliency in the only way she knew how. The nature of that resiliency was one about which she was as ashamed as she was proud.

From the start of the individual psychotherapy, RB noticed and commented on Annie's powerful survival skills. She knew that he knew he might not do as well with her life as she had done. He knew that it would be presumptuous of him to suggest that she might do better by starting over, in effect, in finding ways to cope with an abusive and neglectful family life. He understood that the only thing that was humane, respectful, and practical was to treat her adaptation as a work in progress. He could only hope that she would ultimately choose a less dangerous way of using her resourcefulness to maintain continuity and integrity of self.

It is important to convey in every communication, and at all levels of communication, a respectful understanding of the power of traumatic experiences and the extreme ways of coping that they call forth. This understanding must come without a requirement that survivors be able to speak directly about this. It was incumbent on RB to understand, and to communicate that understanding, that it was Annie's way of being above it all to believe herself invulnerable on her silo lookout, or walking the beams as a welder without restraints, or flying down some back road on her Harley. It is only with this kind of response that a survivor can hold on to an empathic construction of how what happened to her as a child has continued to be a driving force in her life. Once such an empathic construction is more or less in place, it can fuel a process where behavior becomes less driven, and a more moderate solution follows from the separation of present and past. The growing sense of agency and worth creates less urgency and intensity around being oneself, a greater possibility for reparative experiences, and a greater capacity for being pleasurably absorbed. In Annie's case, she began, for example, to define her relationship with her husband differently, to evaluate the safety and well-being of her niece, and to take great pleasure in training a colt with the help of a new woman friend.

Annie realized that it was possible to no longer be controlled by what in her childhood was inescapable. She became receptive to modifying behaviors that endangered her life or confused relationships with others, given the context in which the suggestions of modification were made. The individual therapy context opened her capacity for self-respect, which offered a reparative match for her preoccupation with survival.

## Jo

Jo's confusion about what had happened to her as a child resulted in her continual questioning of her reliability as a narrator of her own life story. As confused as she was, she hated the idea of turning to someone else to determine what was real. On the one hand, she fully expected that her trust would be betrayed by others and that she would be *depersonalized* or objectified in interpersonal exchanges. Her father, for example, had often borrowed the sexualized language of pornography, calling her and her sibling "my little gang bangs." Her mother was regularly dismissive of her assertions about her uncle's perpetration of sexual abuse. On the other hand, there was also something frightening about protective attachments that would allow her to see her life in a clearer focus. She was more reluctant than some of the other group members to readily accept the group's belief in, and sadness about, what she seemed to be saying about her life.

Jo's point of view about what she knew and didn't know about what had happened to her as a child continually shifted, leaving her unempathic about her own adjustment in life and often angry at sympathetic others who must have been seen as messengers bearing the bad news. She had begun to notice early on in the individual therapy process that she would critically challenge, almost interrogate, RB about such things as the reliability of memory or the authority of the therapy profession. She tended to do this at times when she would put forward evidence for having been sexually abused, such as describing being kissed inappropriately by her uncle when she was a young girl, or being treated for rectal bleeding as a child, with physical evidence of trauma later being discovered. But her self-scrutiny was far more intense than her scrutiny of her therapists, and she would often examine every thread of therapeutic data so suspiciously that she became blind to information that was obviously significant. For instance, she would describe how when she was sexual with her husband, she would feel really small, had trouble breathing, and would then lose touch with where she was. At the same time, she thought it unreasonable that she could not enjoy sex with her husband as she should. Or she would describe, and then dismiss, how unnerving it was to sleepwalk in the middle of the night, which she would remember like a dream, and to awaken in the shower after a nightmare about being hopelessly dirty. Or she would say how ashamed she felt to tell of the time she found pornography half hidden in her father's room when she was 10 years old, only to take back its significance by arguing that the glaring presence of pornography in her childhood home wasn't really such a big deal at all. If she could believe that it was she who kept messing up, it would protect her from being humiliated or betrayed. You cannot embarrass someone by publicly showing a private or vulnerable side of her if she readily admits to being shameful on her own. And you cannot betray someone if she does not feel she is deserving of trust in the first place.

In individual therapy, RB's emphasis was on *not overlooking information that is knowable,* as opposed to searching for the unknown. He agreed with Jo that there were unanswerable questions and suggested that they clarify what they had observed and experienced directly in therapy, such as Jo's lack of compassion for herself, her fear of betrayal, her report of experiences of terror in flashbacks, and her inability to hold in mind the evidence she did have of being maltreated as a child. By the 4th month of therapy, Jo had settled into

*Naming the Shadows*

was reminded by a nightmare that she had dreaded her uncle's summer visit, how she had been afraid of dying from rectal bleeding as a child, and how she had wished as an adult, while intoxicated, that her husband would hurt and humiliate her with forced anal sex. SR reminded Jo of what she had not held in mind by simply reading back to her the record of what she, Jo, had said in the previous group. The more complex message was that the data would have to come from Jo, that her uncertainty was taken seriously, that her doubt may have served an adaptive function, and that she could rely on a therapeutic process that was predictable. When Jo expressed concern that she would somehow have to buy into a packaged story if she acknowledged she was abused at all, she was reminded that it was the therapeutic *process* that was common to all group members and that she was not expected to rely on the experiences of others to infer what happened to her.

SR's confrontational style carried an underlying message that Jo was grappling with a very confusing set of experiences that she now had the power to master. The obvious honesty and integrity of the work led to mutual respect and affection. There was even some shared laughter at the end of this sequence of interactions when SR pointed out the illogic in what Jo was in effect saying, which was that she had thought of killing herself over a circumstance that had ruined her life but that had never actually happened. There is something about coming out of hiding that is like a breath of fresh air. It was then the group members who, in a chorus of empathic support for Jo's work, offered the final wisdom that summarized the therapeutic bottom line: "There is no way through it but through it."

In Week 12, Jo was much less reluctant to put forward aspects of her childhood that deeply hurt her as she looked back at them now. A discussion of pornography was initiated by one of the other group members, which led to a frank discussion by Jo of how pornography in her childhood home had led to considerable confusion about what it meant to be treated humanely as a female and as a child. During the initial group discussion, SR had asked the members to consider what the relationship might be between pornography and the perpetration of sexual abuse. They came to the conclusion that sexual abuse, from the perspective of the perpetrator, had something to do with "breaking someone in" in the sense of breaking their spirit, but also in the sense of preparing them for the female role of servicing men's sexual needs. They recognized that the portrayal of women and children in pornography was similarly focused on their obediently following someone else, who then takes sexual pleasure in their subservience—like Quint did with Miles. During the discussion, SR was intent on daylighting the fact that the way women and children were treated in pornographic accounts did not, in her mind, represent a reasonable way to treat another human being. Once Jo related her experiences with her father's pornography, however, there was no need to say any more.

Jo said the worst of the pornography were the story books. She remembered one story about a wife who "wouldn't give her husband any," whose husband then gathered his friends to gang rape her. Apparently the wife wasn't terribly bothered, since she had a good night's sleep and was simply a bit bewildered in the morning. Then there was the story of the father who let his friends have sex with his children, and of the father who had sex with his own children, who very much enjoyed it. Jo remembered that the father in the incest story had the same name as her own father. In fact, every time she heard a person's name when she was a child she would associate it with a character from one of the stories. She said it wouldn't have been so bad to have pornography in the house if her mother had taken responsibility for it instead of blaming her and her brother when they were caught reading it, and if her father hadn't used

*Naming the Shadows*

phrases from the stories in conversations with other people in the family. She had thought that all fathers talked like that. She said she understood now why she had never said anything to her father about her uncle's abuse.

In the next two months of treatment, Jo began to address lingering questions related to her childhood summertime. She reflected on having very fond feelings toward her uncle during extended family gatherings, his playfulness with the children being in contrast to the other adults' unavailability. She recalled him gently holding her in the rocker on the front porch of the family farmhouse alongside her grandmother, whom she admired and loved. She was able to call to mind an incident that left her convinced that her uncle had saved her life. She had been spinning a worm can on her hand as the family was preparing to go fishing, when her uncle noticed a black widow spider on her hand and swatted it off. An image of her beleaguered mother watching reminded her of how she had felt that her uncle loved her more than anyone else did; he was her hero. She also remembered presents her uncle would give her and ask that she keep it secret. She specifically recalled tourist souvenirs and money. His attention had felt both good and bad, and she referred to the gifts as bribes. She understood why she had pretended to be asleep when she heard the screen door slam and heard him approaching in the mornings before her parents came in from the fields for lunch. She understood how she would wish herself away in her imagination to keep her body protected from pain and her mind protected from such irreconcilable betrayal of innocent love.

## Conclusions

The real challenge in trauma-focused psychotherapy is to help survivors to comfortably *be* themselves, initially by seeing themselves through your eyes. This is a real shift in home base from living in the minds of those who have been abusive, or cold and contemptuous, and who have ensured an underlying layer of alienation and help-lessness for those who have had to rely on them. But the power of being oneself in intimate relation to others who truly regard you with warmth and respect, is enough to change the rhythm of life. We are reminded of a survivor who characterized, in a musical metaphor, what it was like to have gotten to the heart of what had been chipping away at her life. It was like soul rhythm and blues.

If, as a therapist, you can find your way through a maze of com-plex communications from the survivor and a way to speak compas-sionately in return, the reward lies in her renewed enthusiasm for embracing life. This is not to say that there is not enormous grief in facing a painful reality about one's personal history, even with the realization that the present holds possibilities different from the past. And it is not to say that all symptoms and problems in living will simply disappear. But to allow someone the perspective that comes from joining a group of onlookers who are truly interested in what's going on is to allow the possibility of transforming the worst of what human relatedness has to offer into meaningful commit-ments that hold the best of human values in mind.

In the lives of the survivors we have discussed so far, as well as the two who remain to be introduced, there was no one to provide the strength, compassion, and perspective necessary to ensure that the *meaning* attached to the abusive experiences limited rather than magnified the negative impact of the abusive experiences. The sur-vivors of our study had also been denied respectful listening for decades, partly because of peoples' need for denial of the impact of childhood sexual trauma, but also perhaps because of an overzeal-ous desire to help by some who were unable to provide the appropri-ate social context (such as Miles's governess). For the survivors in our study, a therapeutic framework was needed to bring to light the traumatic meanings that characterized their adaptation and lived in the current representations that structured their world.

We have emphasized issues of self and social definition that are based in the traumatic experiences, because we believe that the wide array of symptoms associated with sexual abuse are best contextualized in this way. As we shift, in the next chapter, to a consideration of quantitative changes in symptoms and trauma themes over the course of the year-long psychotherapy, we are making certain assumptions that we should be explicit about now. We would argue that it is the reflective appraisal of the trauma memory in the social context of the psychotherapy that leads to an understanding of the trauma's current presence or influence, as well as to an understanding of its initial impact in the past. This leads to a clearer understanding on all levels of experience that the past is past and to a consequent undermining of the outdated PTSD states of mind and related symptoms. Not only is there less reaction to the trauma in terms of intrusive, avoidant, or hypervigilant states once the trauma is "seen" and put in its place, but there is also better regulation of affect, impulses, and consciousness that results from the reduced potential for the trauma memory to be automatically and uncontrollably called to mind. The reflective appraisal, finally, leads to a very different understanding about what happened, an understanding that lifts a tremendous burden of shameful feelings and leads to a revised personal theory of reality that both incorporates the trauma and allows for a broader enjoyment of life.

# Chapter 3

# A Self-Study of Therapeutic Efficacy

The ideal context in which to do psychotherapeutic work is one where there is an ongoing systematic evaluation of the efficacy of treatment. We call this evaluation a self-study because of the emphasis on *observing ourselves* as therapists, literally, in our case, because we had the resources to record our therapeutic work on video. But even without a picture to aid the process of self-study, one can still achieve a self-conscious attitude about what is being done and what impact it is having on the people in treatment. And to ensure that there is a more objective verification of treatment effects than the subjective impressions of someone with an obvious self-interest in believing in good outcomes, the systematic measurement of markers of improvement provides essential information.

Evaluating both subjectively and objectively on an ongoing basis the outcome of psychotherapy alters the process substantially. Being in the mindset of trying to figure something out, rather than simply implementing something known, creates an energy of innovation and thoughtfulness that enhances the therapeutic work. And the shared self-consciousness between therapist and survivor about the ongoing evaluation of the *therapist* enhances the sense of collaboration in working in the survivor's best interest. With the video cameras pointing at us rather than facing our subjects, there was an important message about *our* responsibility, as well as theirs, in the success of the work. In the context of our self-study, we each had the experience of being at our best as therapists.

Our study was conducted at the training clinic for the Ph.D. program in clinical psychology at Duke University. We enjoyed the advantage of weekly discussions of the therapy process for each of our subjects, which provided the opportunity to observe each other's work as well as our own, and to maximize coordination of our efforts. Student trainees who were working on the project joined our discussions regularly and helped us articulate what it was we were doing that we deemed effective. Although our treatment does not lend itself to the kind of instruction manuals that have been so helpful in the study of cognitive-behavioral techniques, we were able to collect enough case material over the course of the project to enable a clinically rich description of our work.

We observed in our subjects a genuine pride in being a part of our research. They seemed to appreciate the care with which a team of experts was attending to their treatment needs and valued contributing to a knowledge base that would be helpful to other survivors in the future. The constraints on the length of treatment resulting from the research protocol served as additional motivation to work harder to achieve positive outcomes within a year.

In this chapter, we will describe the methods and quantitative results of our self-study in the hope of modeling what we believe is an important element of clinical practice. Our data on markers of improvement in response to our treatment are also interesting in their own right. Because of our small sample of study participants, and the absence of a control group of any kind, our data are only suggestive of central tendencies that could be expected with a larger sample of similar subjects. We are nevertheless extremely encouraged by the findings of our systematic clinical assessments and are reassured by their consistency with what we observed in our more subjective tracking of individual cases.

For those readers who are less concerned with the details of the research process, we have included a section entitled "Summary of Findings of the Self-Study" to which they can directly turn. For all readers, following the summary, we have contextualized our measurement of posttraumatic symptoms and themes in descriptions of our study participants Caroline and Alice. Our intention here is to illustrate how the quantitative data bear on our conceptualization of the treatment process in individual cases.

## Methods of the Incest Self-Study

The intention of our study was to scrutinize what we felt was our best-shot treatment effort. Our best shot was a multimodal approach that included individual therapy, group therapy, and pharmacotherapy. We initially attempted to independently recruit survivors with an interest in being treated by pharmacotherapy alone, in order to have some point of comparison for the effects of psychotherapy. We were unsuccessful in recruiting, however, and tentatively concluded that incest survivors meeting the study criteria described below do not routinely self-select into drug treatment. This lack of success in finding interested subjects for drug treatment was consistent with our long-standing clinical experience: Incest survivors who seek therapy are looking for some understanding about who they are as much as they are looking for relief from symptoms.

While the improvement we observed in response to our treatment could have been due to a variety of specific factors or combinations of factors, the passage of time is one explanation for change that we do not find plausible. Keep in mind that our subjects were dealing with a chronic set of problems related to childhood trauma and that they had all previously been involved in at least one other trauma-focused psychotherapy. It is also clear from the quantitative as well as the qualitative data that the pharmacotherapy treatment alone could not plausibly account for the changes we observed. We do not know, however, to what extent it contributed to the effectiveness of our psychotherapy.

### Our Sample of Incest Survivors

At the time of the study, both of us enjoyed a long-standing reputation in our community for the respectful treatment of trauma survivors. Furthermore, the Duke Psychology Clinic that would house the study had a fine reputation for training and service in the domain of trauma-focused psychotherapy. Announcements sent to local therapists, victim advocacy agencies, and newspapers resulted, in the subsequent 2½ months, in calls from 62 women interested in treatment. Our focus on *female* survivors reflected our greater psychotherapy expertise with females and our desire to have an all-women's group. We have no reason to believe, however, that our treatment approach would be unsuitable for male survivors of childhood incest.

Only a relatively small percentage of callers, approximately 13%, maintained interest in our study and also met our criteria for participating. Our goal was to include subjects 21 years of age and older who believed they had been sexually abused as children by someone in their family, who carried a related and current posttraumatic stress disorder diagnosis, who had not experienced any sexual trauma (e.g., sexual assault) in the past year, who were reasonable candidates for our chosen drug treatment, who could safely engage in our psychotherapy within a 1-year time frame, and who were willing to terminate any current treatment. Slightly over half of the callers excluded themselves from treatment after making contact with us, many for financial reasons, or out of concern for the pharmacotherapy component of treatment. Approximately an additional third of the callers were excluded by us, mostly out of our concern for their ability to benefit from our treatment. Many of these callers were dealing with a recent or ongoing traumatic situation, or had been recently hospitalized, or evidenced mistrustful and hostile behavior, or were highly dissociative. While we were cautious about only including survivors who we were confident could handle the intensity of our interventions, we did not routinely exclude subjects on the basis of any single criteria. Our sample included, for example, 1 subject with a prior psychiatric hospitalization (Caroline), and 2 subjects who had made suicide attempts as teenagers (Jesse and Annie). In all cases, we judged the people in our sample to be capable of both forming and tolerating the loss of secure attachments with the therapists. For a more detailed description of the initial screening process, as well as a detailed description of the methods and quantitative results of our project, see Turner, DeRosa, Roth, Batson, and Davidson (1996).

We began our study in earnest with 8 survivors. One of our subjects withdrew from the study before the treatment began, and another subject withdrew from the study after 6 months. The 6 remaining survivors, 5 white and 1 Asian-American woman, ranging in age from 26 to 40, comprise our sample. All the survivors had at least some college education, and 4 of the 6 had advanced degrees, making our sample far more educated than the population norm. Five of our subjects came to a confident conclusion about their abuse in the course of treatment, and our 6th subject (Alice), while convinced that she had been sexually abused, remained tentative as to the identity of the perpetrator. In addition to enduring incest, the survivors in our sample endured other traumas as well, including complicated bereavement, serious accidents, sexual and/or physical assaults by perpetrators outside of the family of origin, and physical abuse as a child within the family context.

While our sample was highly educated and relatively high functioning, they were also highly traumatized, which was reflected in the extent to which they met criteria for psychiatric diagnoses. Everyone in the sample had, either at the time of initiation of the study or previously, expressed the symptoms for at least two other psychiatric diagnoses in addition to posttraumatic stress disorder. Everyone in the sample at some point carried a diagnosis of major depression, and two-thirds of the sample at some point carried a diagnosis of panic disorder. Other than mood disorders and anxiety disorders, eating disorders, substance use disorders, and Axis II disorders were each represented in a third of our sample.

## The Multimodal Treatment Protocol

The individual psychotherapy was developed and conducted by the second author (RB). Each of the 6 study participants received 1 hour of individual psychotherapy per week over the course of a 12-month period. The concurrent group psychotherapy, developed and conducted by the first author (SR), met for 2 consecutive hours each week, and included a graduate student cotherapist whose role was predominantly observational. As mentioned previously, 1 of the 6 members of our sample, Annie, completed only half the year of the group treatment, while completing the year of individual psychotherapy. Psychotherapy was provided to all survivors at a substantial reduction of standard fees.

The pharmacotherapy treatment protocol was developed by Dr. Jonathan Davidson of Duke University Medical Center. The protocol is consistent with standard clinical practice and is available from Dr. Davidson upon request. Fluoxetine (Prozac) was added to the

## A Self-Study of Therapeutic Efficacy

treatment program to deintensify the initial response to approaching traumatic material. Posttraumatic symptoms have been shown to respond particularly well to drugs with serotoninergic properties, including fluoxetine (see Turner et al., 1996), and it is preferable to complement psychotherapy with pharmacotherapy when feasible, in our opinion. Fluoxetine was administered in the context of individual psychotherapy by RB, beginning with a 10-mg daily dosage. The dosage was gradually increased for all participants until there was judged to be maximum benefit without troubling side effects. The range of the maintenance doses for the sample was 30–50 mg per day. Medication was provided free of charge to study participants.

All participants were aware at the outset that the treatment program would terminate at the end of a year. They were told that if further psychotherapy was seen as desirable, continuation of individual therapy could be provided after the 3-month posttermination follow-up assessment. One person (Alice) expressed an interest in continuing psychotherapy at the time of termination, and she resumed individual therapy with RB after the collection of data at the 3-month follow-up. Pharmacotherapy was continued into the follow-up period for Alice, Jo, and Annie.

### Clinical Assessment: The Markers of Improvement

Participants in our study were evaluated by a graduate student trainee prior to treatment, at 6 months into treatment and at termination, and twice during the 6-month posttermination period. The purpose of the evaluations was to obtain, by structured clinical interview, information pertaining to psychiatric diagnoses, particularly PTSD, as well as information pertaining to symptoms of Complex PTSD and to trauma themes. The structured clinical interview for DSM-III-R (SCID-I and II for Axis I and II disorders) is the gold standard assessment interview for psychiatric diagnosis, which we relied on exclusively for all diagnostic assessment except that regarding PTSD. For PTSD, we relied on a widely used structured interview, the SI-PTSD designed by Dr. Jonathan Davidson, which provided a severity rating for each symptom (see Turner et al., 1996, for a more complete description of these structured interviews). Our assessment of Complex PTSD symptoms and trauma themes, as described in chapter 1, was completed at the same time as the diagnostic assessments, creating more of a context of meaningful conversation from which needed information was abstracted.

## Quantitative Changes in Symptoms and Trauma Themes

The overall improvement on our objective measures of treatment effectiveness was consistent with what we observed in the way of personal transformations of the legacy of childhood abuse. We are particularly interested in a closer look at posttraumatic stress disorder symptoms, at the constellation of symptoms we call complex posttraumatic stress disorder, and at the trauma themes that reflect one's personal theory of reality and form the bridge, in our view, between the reflective appraisal of the trauma memory and the reduction of symptoms. We will not discuss in any depth the changes we measured in regard to symptoms of other Axis I and II disorders that were comorbid with PTSD at the start of treatment. However, we do want to mention that there was significant clinical improvement in this arena in our sample as well. The effect of our work on a broad range of symptoms and disorders convinces us further of the importance of contextualizing psychiatric symptoms in a complete understanding of the traumatic imprint. Figure 3–1 provides a quantitative look at the improvement in Axis I disorders other than PTSD for the sample as a whole over the course of the treatment and follow-up. The Axis II disorders initially present in our sample,

A Self-Study of Therapeutic Efficacy

**FIGURE 3–1**

*Mean Number of Axis I Comorbid Disorders*

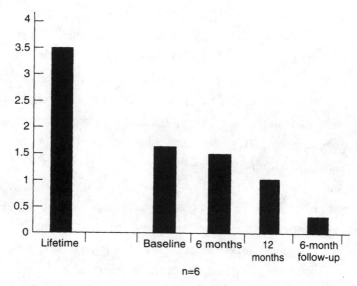

obsessive-compulsive personality disorder and dependent personality disorder, similarly improved with treatment. In the sample as a whole, while the major categories of symptoms persisted to some extent after treatment, they were substantially less prominent.

## Posttraumatic Stress Disorder

The structured interview for posttraumatic stress disorder allows a trained interviewer to rate each of 17 symptoms on a scale from 0 to 4, with 1 indicating *mild,* and 4 indicating *extremely severe* distress resulting from the symptom. Zero indicates absence of the symptom. There are 5 intrusive, 7 avoidant, and 5 hyperarousal symptoms in all, and for a DSM-IV (APA, 1994) diagnosis of posttraumatic stress disorder to be present, 1 intrusive, 3 avoidant, and 2 hyperarousal symptoms must be rated 2 or higher. An overall severity rating for the group of symptoms can be established, as well as severity ratings for each of the 3 clusters.

*Naming the Shadows*

Finally, each symptom can be given a severity rating that indicates the worst it's ever been, as well as how bad it was in the past 4 weeks.

Figure 3–2 illustrates the substantial improvement in PTSD symptoms by picturing the level of distress ratings summed across symptoms and averaged across subjects. The level of distress for symptoms at their worst is indicated, as well as the severity ratings made over the course of treatment and through the follow-up period. While all members of our sample met criteria for PTSD at the baseline assessment, only 2 members (Caroline and Alice) met criteria at any of the 3 assessments from termination through the 6-month posttermination point. One of the subjects, Caroline, no longer met diagnostic criteria at either 3 or 6 months posttermination. Taking the 3 assessments from termination through the 6-month posttermination point as a whole, there was approximately a 50% improvement in severity or level of distress of symptoms over baseline level.

If one looks more closely at the data from the SI-PTSD, by considering the mean *number* of symptoms endorsed over time, in addition to the level of distress across symptoms that is pictured in Figure 3–2, it is clear that what is improving is the number of symptoms endorsed, as opposed to the typical level of distress at which any particular symptom is rated. Thus, while the mean number of PTSD symptoms endorsed by the subjects in our sample dropped approximately 50% between baseline and the posttreatment period, from approximately 12 to 6, the average severity or level of distress rating *per symptom* remained essentially the same at around a rating of 3.

If we look at the mean level of distress for each of the three PTSD symptom clusters separately (see Figures 3–3, 3–4 and 3–5), and again consider the 6-month posttreatment period as a whole, we see that there was a similar degree of improvement across time in each case, with the avoidant symptoms showing the greatest change, and

A Self-Study of Therapeutic Efficacy

**FIGURE 3–2**

*Mean Level of Total PTSD Symptoms (68 possible)*

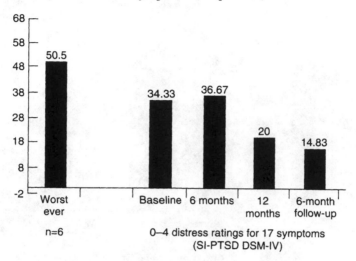

n=6

0–4 distress ratings for 17 symptoms
(SI-PTSD DSM-IV)

**FIGURE 3–3**

*Mean Level of Intrusive PTSD Symptoms (20 possible)*

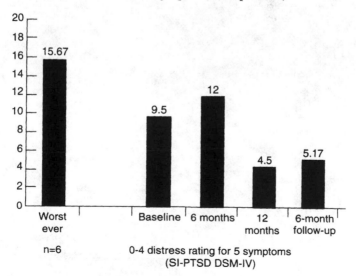

n=6

0-4 distress rating for 5 symptoms
(SI-PTSD DSM-IV)

**FIGURE 3–4**

*Mean Level of Avoidant PTSD Symptoms (28 possible)*

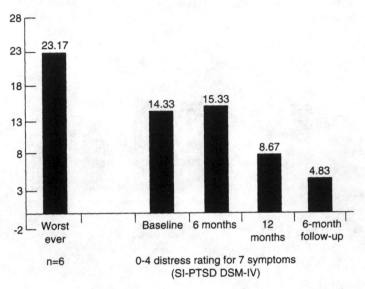

**FIGURE 3–5**

*Mean Level of Arousal PTSD Symptoms (20 possible)*

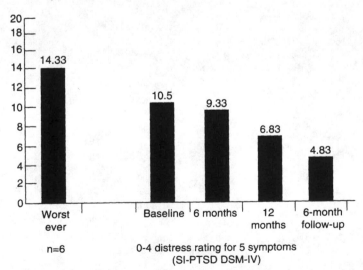

the intrusive symptoms the least. Remember in viewing the graphs that the maximum level of distress for intrusive and arousal symptoms is not the same as it is for avoidance symptoms because of the different number of symptoms in the clusters. For all PTSD figures, the 3-month follow-up point is not represented.

Another finding that is consistent with our clinical impressions in this study, and with our broader clinical experience over the years, is the increase, at 6 months into treatment, in the level of distress for intrusive and avoidant symptoms. This increase in symptom severity occurs *despite* the medication regimen and probably *because of* the psychotherapy. To move into a different relationship to traumatic material by taking it on and wrestling with it is not a small accomplishment, and the psychotherapeutic process is extremely painful at times for everyone, especially in the initial stages prior to any sense of an evolving mastery. It is not until well into the psychotherapy that some symptomatic benefit begins to appear, but there is no way, in our view, to expedite this. Again, we believe that the symptomatic relief comes from the deeper transformation of meaning attached to traumatic experiences, and even when we provide help from all sides, this transformation takes time.

We believe that most survivors continue to grapple with the traumatic impact of incest as they progress through adult development and encounter new roles and new relationships. What needs to be in place prior to concluding therapy are the resources and confidence to continue to engage a process similar to the therapeutic one on one's own or with the help of intimate friends. The persistence of PTSD symptoms in our sample at the end of treatment did not convince us of the need for a longer treatment for most survivors who have the same resources as our subjects. We were, on the contrary, reassured about the success of our termination of the psychotherapy by the fact that gains made in

*Naming the Shadows*

regard to PTSD symptoms were, on average, sustained over the 6-month follow-up period. The reduction in PTSD symptoms that was observed by the end of psychotherapy was a reflection of the changing force of the trauma itself in the current lives of the survivors, a force over which they had at that point achieved considerable control.

## Complex Posttraumatic Stress Disorder

The structured clinical interview for the evaluation of symptoms associated with Complex PTSD resulted in the rating of the presence or absence, in the previous 4 weeks, of symptoms in each of the 7 categories and 27 subcategories indicated previously in chapter 1. The total number of symptoms endorsed across all categories, and averaged across subjects, for each of four time periods is indicated in Figure 3–6. As can be seen, these associated features of PTSD "be-

**FIGURE 3–6**

*Mean Number of Complex PTSD Symptoms*

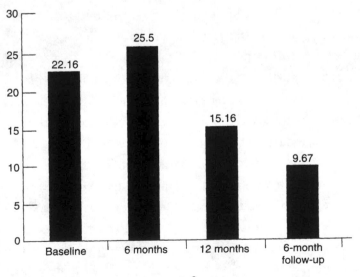

n=6

*A Self-Study of Therapeutic Efficacy*

haved" very much the same as the PTSD symptoms proper, with approximately a 50% reduction over the course of treatment.

The most parsimonious way to consider these data more thoroughly is to observe the percent change in average symptom endorsement for each of the major symptom categories separately. In Figure 3–7 the number of symptoms endorsed in each of 6 categories, averaged across subjects, was compared between baseline and the three endpoints on average (12 months, 3-month follow-up, and 6-month follow-up).

As can be seen in the figure, the percent reduction in symptoms is quite variable and could reflect a number of factors. Whether some symptoms are simply more resistant to change, or less responsive to our

**FIGURE 3–7**

*Percent Reduction in Mean Number of Complex PTSD Symptoms (baseline through average posttermination)*

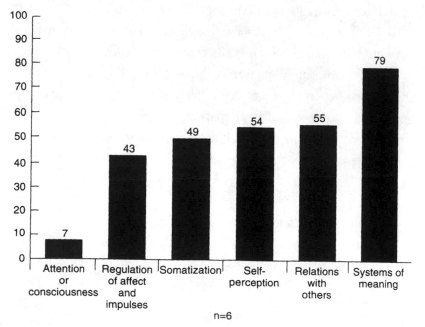

n=6

particular intervention, is not clear to us. We view these data as a preliminary indication of differential reactivity of symptom clusters that might generate interesting hypotheses for further study. For example, the categories of symptoms that were most directly targeted by our psychotherapy, Self-Perception, Relations with Others, and Systems of Meaning, showed the greatest improvement. Regulation of Affect and Impulses and Somatization were not far behind in improvement, however, and only symptoms of amnesia, dissociation, and depersonalization (Attention or Consciousness) did not substantially change. Unfortunately, there is no way to establish the reliability of observed mean differences due to the small size of our sample. Further research is also required to firmly establish the validity of the 6 symptom clusters. Again, our results are only suggestive of true differences. The category of symptoms not included in the figure, Perception of the Perpetrator, was not seen as particularly relevant for our sample of incest survivors, and was also judged, in previous studies reported in chapter 1, to not be central to the overall set of Complex PTSD symptoms.

We have presented in Table 3–1 a characterization of each of the 6 symptom clusters represented in Figure 3–7. In the actual clinical interview, a symptom was rated as "present" if the behavior or emotional reaction was judged to be clinically significant because of subjective distress, social and occupational impairment, or considerations of frequency. In the original conceptualization of the symptoms, as described in chapter 1, the observed *co-occurrence* of the 6 clusters in trauma victims was considered to be clinically significant, and preliminary diagnostic criteria were established for further study. In our study sample, 4 of our subjects met these preliminary diagnostic criteria for complex posttraumatic stress disorder during the first 6 months of treatment, and all 4 no longer met criteria by some point in the posttermination period.

**TABLE 3–1**

*Characterization of Complex
Posttraumatic Stress Disorder Symptoms*

*Regulation of Affect and Impulses*—Characterized by emotional hyperreactivity, especially with regard to anger, deliberate or inadvertent self-harm or excessive risk taking, and driven or avoidant behaviors relating to sexuality.

*Attention or Consciousness*—Characterized by difficulty maintaining a coherent life narrative and sense of continuity of self over the short-term as well as the long-term.

*Self-Perception*—Characterized by experiences of self as damaged, lacking in agency, shameful, and alienated from one's social context.

*Relations with Others*—Characterized by an inability to trust people, an avoidance of relationships, difficulty working through interpersonal conflicts, and a vulnerability to inadvertently repeat aspects of childhood abusive relationships in current relationships.

*Somatization*—Characterized by somatic symptoms for which a physical cause has not been found.

*Systems of Meaning*—Characterized by pessimism about the future with regard to relationships and meaningful work and to matters broadly defined as spiritual.

## Trauma Themes

At each of the evaluation points, our subjects were rated on the trauma themes described in chapter 1. They were also rated on a catchall theme of "diffuse affect," which included intense emotions not otherwise classifiable, such as pain, misery, discomfort, or hurt. All in all, there were 15 themes evaluated during the interviews, at which time our study participants reflected on the current meaning of their traumatic experiences and offered their evolving perspective on how it affected their lives. For each theme, our raters made a clinical judgment regarding the degree of resolution of that theme according to the dimensions described in chapter 1. Our highest ratings of 5 and 6, which we group as indicating *resolution,* were given in those instances where a successful process had been engaged to limit the negative impact of abuse. Our highest ratings presumed an awareness on the survivor's part of how the particular theme was associated with the circumstances of an abusive childhood, such as an awareness that being quick to anger was related to a deep-seated rage about one's abuse and about the general lack of protection in family life. Our highest ratings also required the ability on the survivor's part to cut the abusive experience down to size, such as an ability to focus on one's competencies, or pride in accomplishments, or positive connections with other people, and so on. In effect, resolution was indicated by a realization on a survivor's part that her experience of living in a context where abuse persisted should not define the full potential of her experience into the future.

For each individual, a particular theme was considered to be *unresolved* if it received a rating lower than 5. Ratings of 1 were very uncommon, and ratings of 2 only slightly more common in this group of survivors, even at baseline. For the most part, thematic material targeted in treatment was in the survivor's conscious awareness. The therapeutic effect occurred in an understanding of the traumatic origin of the experiences described by the themes, followed by a reconstruction of the implication of what happened in childhood for representations of the self, others, and the world in the present.

In Figure 3–8 the theme scores over time, averaged across themes and subjects, are represented; in Figure 3–9 the number of unresolved themes, averaged across subjects, is represented at the four time periods. In both cases it is clear that there is a steady improvement in theme resolution over the course of treatment, as well as

*A Self-Study of Therapeutic Efficacy*

into the follow-up period, which represents substantial clinical change. Perhaps the apparent general improvement in both themes and symptoms into the follow-up period simply reflects a 12-month data point that is somewhat unrepresentative of the degree of treatment effectiveness, due to the stress of termination at that time. It is also plausible that our subjects continued to benefit from a process set in motion in treatment, which enabled the ongoing adaptive reconstruction of meaning.

If we look at the average change over time in individual themes, there is substantial clinical change for all themes, and also considerable variability among the themes. The clearest way to compare the change across themes is with a percentage of the maximum

**FIGURE 3–8**

*Average Theme Score*

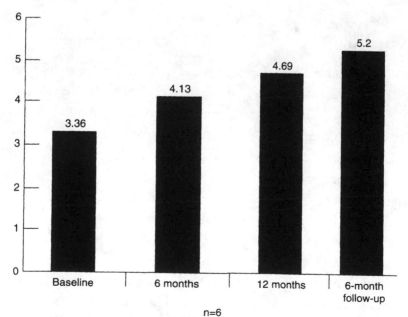

n=6

**FIGURE 3–9**

*Mean Number of Unresolved Themes (15 possible)*

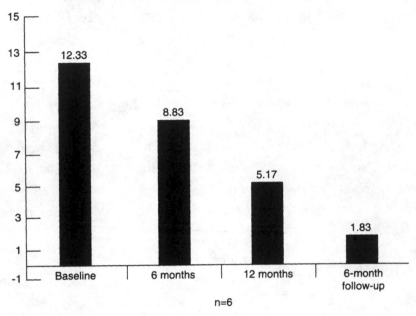

change possible. A theme that went from a 4 to a 5 would get a score of 50%, since it was halfway to a score of 6, the maximum. In Figure 3–10 change is averaged across subjects and represents the time period from baseline to the averaged posttermination points (12 months, 3-month follow-up, and 6-month follow-up). In the accompanying table, the actual theme scores, averaged across subjects, are listed for baseline, 6 months, and the posttermination period. Using this data set as a stimulus for hypotheses generation, we wonder whether the apparent relative difficulty in resolving such themes as guilt and shame, compared with such themes as alienation and meaningful world, has to do with the developmental sequencing of experiences in response to chronic abuse, the degree to which experiences are under cognitive control, or the relevance of

**FIGURE 3–10**

*Percent of Maximum Improvement in Average Theme Score for 15 Themes (baseline through average posttermination, n=6)*

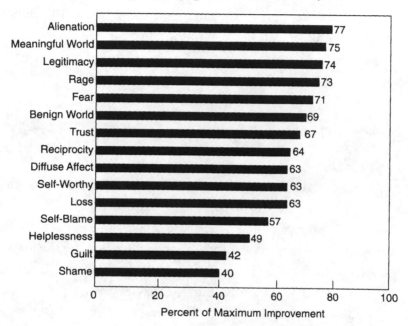

Percent of Maximum Improvement

**TABLE 3–2**

|          | Baseline | 6 Months | Postterm. |          | Baseline | 6 Months | Postterm. |
|----------|----------|----------|-----------|----------|----------|----------|-----------|
| Alien.   | 3.6      | 3.67     | 5.45      | Diff. Aff. | 3.6    | 4.0      | 5.11      |
| Mean. W. | 3.83     | 4.5      | 5.45      | Self-W.  | 3.33     | 4.0      | 5.0       |
| Legit.   | 2.83     | 4.33     | 5.17      | Loss     | 3.17     | 3.5      | 4.95      |
| Rage     | 2.5      | 4.33     | 5.06      | Self-Bl. | 3.17     | 4.17     | 4.77      |
| Fear     | 3.33     | 4.0      | 5.22      | Help.    | 3.83     | 4.67     | 4.89      |
| Ben. W.  | 3.83     | 4.5      | 5.33      | Guilt    | 3.5      | 3.5      | 4.56      |
| Trust    | 3.17     | 4.33     | 5.06      | Shame    | 3.5      | 3.67     | 4.5       |
| Recip.   | 3.4      | 4.83     | 5.06      |          |          |          |           |

nontrauma-related experiences to a modification of the significance of the abuse. Perhaps shame, for example, is not so easily reevaluated, even if there is a genuine experience of pride in oneself that is established in the course of therapy and a clear understanding of the perpetrator's responsibility for the abuse. Even shame, though, showed substantial improvement by the posttermination period.

## Summary of Findings of the Self-Study

In our sample as a whole, there was significant clinical improvement in symptoms of the Axis I and Axis II disorders that were comorbid with PTSD in our sample at the start of treatment. For PTSD and Complex PTSD symptoms, there was approximately a 50% improvement in severity of symptoms over baseline level by the follow-up period. An initial increase in severity of PTSD and Complex PTSD symptoms at 6 months into treatment was consistent with our broader clinical experience of the therapeutic process as difficult and painful, and requiring at least a year-long time frame.

Movement in trauma theme resolution was steady over the course of the treatment and through the follow-up period and represented substantial clinical change. The therapeutic effect in regard to trauma themes occurred for the most part in our subjects' understanding of the traumatic origins of their fear, shame, alienation, or rage, and then in a reconstruction of the meaning of the childhood abuse and how they thought about themselves and their social world in the present.

We are generally impressed with the consistency of our markers of improvement in the areas represented by psychiatric diagnoses, trauma themes, and Complex PTSD symptoms to demonstrate significant clinical change within 1 year. Although our subjects were not free of symptoms by our last evaluation of them 6 months after the termination of treatment, the context for the symptoms had substantially changed. It is fair to characterize the group of survivors as no longer having the experience of themselves as psychologically deviant or unworthy of love, or as driven by anger over past betrayals. Rather, as the therapy drew to a close, they saw before them a social world with different possibilities than were held by the past, and they had begun to engage that world with a sense of agency and hope for meaningful relationships.

In concluding the first half of the book, we now introduce our remaining study subjects, Caroline and Alice, with the goal of illustrating the manner in which we use our quantitative data in individual cases. Contextualizing Caroline's and Alice's posttraumatic symptom and theme ratings in a fuller understanding of their adaptations keeps us true to our stated commitment to always keep this "bigger picture" of the traumatic adaptation in mind.

## Caroline

Approximately 6 months into treatment, RB and Caroline together reviewed the hospital and office records of Caroline's psychotherapeutic treatment by her prior therapist. Caroline had been hospitalized at the age of 30 for 2 weeks approximately 2½ years prior to the beginning of treatment in our study. According to the records, she had become somewhat depressed after the birth of her daughter 8 months earlier, and became more acutely distressed after her brother's suicide three months prior to her hospitalization. She reported having a long history of panic attacks, and upon her hospitalization her thinking was disorganized, and she was obsessed with sexual thoughts and the possibility of having been sexually abused. Her severe confusion led to the conclusion by her therapist that her symptoms represented a brief psychotic reaction. Sexual abuse remained a working hypothesis and likelihood for both Caroline and her therapist throughout treatment. After a 2-week hospital stay, Caroline continued treatment as an outpatient up to approximately 6 months prior to the beginning of our study. This earlier treatment was, in our view, successful in helping Caroline begin to see her confusion as a source of meaningful information.

Caroline's confusion about her personal history had intensified for the first time after the birth of her daughter. The profound grief over the suicide of her younger brother 5 months later further contributed to an urgency about establishing confidence in her ability to protect herself and her daughter from harm. This urgency seems quite adaptive in hindsight, as it provided the impetus to clarify her own experiences in a way that would enable her to more easily provide her child with the safety and nurture of which she, Caroline, had been deprived. Unfortunately, she did not see her life course as adaptive, and she experienced intense shame over her confusion, the hospitalization, and the fragmentary memories she reflected on over the course of treatment. Shame was the most difficult theme for Caroline to resolve.

In general, Caroline's improvement in symptoms and trauma themes during our treatment was somewhat above the average of our group of survivors. Her panic symptoms were no longer diagnostically significant 6 months into treatment, and PTSD and Complex PTSD were no longer diagnostically significant by the posttreatment follow-up. The change in her themes scores, furthermore, indicated great success in limiting the power of the abusive experiences to affectively drive or otherwise define current-day living and future hopes and plans. That Caroline, like other survivors, continued to suffer from some trauma-related symptoms at our last evaluation was not really disturbing in the context of her newly developed confidence in, and gentleness toward, herself. Her confidence in her perceptions and her empathic view toward what she had been through were perhaps the most significant changes during treatment from both our perspective and hers.

Caroline's treatment in individual therapy was focused on teaching her to reflectively view her symptoms and her confusion as *meaningful* parts of her trauma memory, which "speak in disguised language of secrets too terrible for words" and which both "reveal and conceal their origins" (Herman, 1992, p. 96). RB persistently talked about her symptoms as the creations of a survivalist, evoking the sense of her as the healthy author of a cleverly camouflaged life narrative. In both the individual and group psychotherapy, it was made clear that what she recalled about what happened to her was not a marker of success. Reflecting on her experiences in the present, on the ever-present but overlooked trauma memory, was the task. Even her amnesia was viewed as adaptive, not shameful, because there was an assumption that in the therapeutic context she would have the ability to regulate what she could tolerate fully knowing and actually articulating. Rather than placing a value on certainty, we encouraged her to take some comfort in uncertainty, an attitude that profoundly eased the task of finding a meaningful way of viewing her personal history. Again, as therapists, we are required to have a deep respect for the power of childhood trauma to overwhelm and disorganize personality, even when there is no longer objective danger present. That is not to say that it is impossible to understand the trauma imprint without exposing the fully detailed trauma story.

Caroline had experienced at times a sense of pride and power in her precocious knowledge of sexuality, reactions that seemed largely in defense of her fear and humiliation surrounding early childhood sexual preoccupations and responses. Her confusion surrounding these childhood memories was intensified by intrusive images and sounds relating to sexualized danger at the hands of her father. In the present, her father routinely offered his opinion that Caroline was crazy, while at the same time disapproving of her seeking any psychological help. Caroline's parents had generally found ways over the years of magically turning her pride regarding her accomplishments, her talents, her resourcefulness, or her integrity into shame. She told a poignant story of having made a decorative bread board for her mother at school, which her mother then broke on her bottom while beating her. In general, pursuing her own interests was seen as an insult, an injury, or an instance of disloyalty by her parents. It was no wonder that she constantly feared that they would somehow find a way to destroy her pride in being an exemplary mother to her little girl.

The late Silvan Tomkins, a brilliant authority on affect, describes shame as an inner torment, striking deepest into the human heart, "a sickness of the soul" (1963, p. 118). With Caroline you could often feel her shame, as in the way she would be so grateful for the small kindnesses that most people take for granted. We are reminded of one particular night in group, when she was full of sorrow over her brother's death and her parents' cruelty. She began to express her anxiety about her parents finding some way to take her daughter from her, and she kept using the same small piece of tissue over and over again as she cried, as if caught in a spell of her unworthiness. An offer by SR that she could have her own new box of tissues seemed to break the power of her shame and bring into awareness the compassion surrounding her in the room. With Caroline you could also often feel her warmth and ease of intimate connection. She and the other members of the group had a good laugh that night about the tissues, in appreciation of an outdated burden losing its hold.

*A Self-Study of Therapeutic Efficacy*

We believe Caroline was deeply grateful to the therapists and the group members for giving her the encouragement and confidence to take pride in her ability to care for herself and her daughter. By bringing the trauma memory into focus, Caroline came to understand the current presence of her childhood trauma, as well as its impact in the past. This understanding was the antidote to her confusion, and allowed her to feel secure in her competencies, as well as respectful of the role of her continued amnesia. Her persistent symptoms, in general, were less shameful in the context of her new understanding of their origins and her sound identification with other survivors.

## Alice

Despite many years of prior psychotherapy, Alice was highly symptomatic upon entering treatment with us. She met diagnostic criteria for a number of Axis I and II disorders in addition to PTSD and Complex PTSD. Although her improvement on trauma themes was steady over the course of treatment, the percent change in theme scores from baseline lagged behind the average gain in our sample as a whole, and by the time of termination, there remained a substantial number of unresolved themes. While her psychiatric symptoms, including PTSD symptoms, also improved significantly over the course of treatment, there was evidence for a reversal in improvement in regard to some symptoms over the posttreatment period. We were generally satisfied that the treatment was having some benefit and that the process had been solidly engaged by Alice, but we believed there was need for further treatment in order for gains to be sustained, as well as for further progress to be achieved. Alice reentered therapy with RB approximately 3 months after concluding the year-long trial.

We will describe here only the work that occurred during the initial year of treatment in the context of our study.

In the week prior to the beginning of our study, Alice described an intensification of revivifications of childhood traumatic experiences. These revivifications amplified her worries about maintaining her ability to function if she were to understand what had happened to her as a child. In fact, her adaptation to what seemed to be an extremely chaotic childhood family life was to obfuscate the possibility of a clear narrative by using her intellect and imagination to design her own unsolvable puzzles. Her waking associations that she tried to make sense of often included images that were dreamlike and symbolic, and her attempt at analysis of these images often led to an impressive array of contradictory hypotheses that were difficult to sort out. Toward the end of the study, the redundant style and thematic content of her metaphoric communication made it easier to reflect on traumatic material, and some clarity was starting to emerge in regard to her trauma memory. A great deal of uncertainty remained, however, even with respect to the "big picture," as well as the more specific questions that Alice had brought to treatment at the outset, or had generated in the early months of the study. This uncertainty attenuated an appreciation, by Alice, of a less shameful adaptiveness, competence, and control.

Alice's imagery reflected an affective intensity that matched in extremity her lack of direct emotional expressiveness in both individual and group therapy. For example, when asked to reflect on how she was feeling, she might describe a child inside her throat trying to slice her vocal cords with a knife, or she and a group of girls of different ages "being sucked toward something like the internal propeller of a jet engine." Or what she came to understand as her mother's coldness, volatility, and sexualized demeanor had been represented in a repetitive image of her made-up, red lipsticked mother with her high heel pressing Alice against the floor. Alice was telling us in the best way she could about her emotional life. The passion of positive emotions that she said she could not feel inside of her seemed safely locked away, for the most part, with her rage and fear, and also with her grief at the thought of her father's betrayal. Even when she did experience emotional suffering, it was somehow separated from the therapeutic work and also from the sphere of connection in her attachments with her therapists.

Alice was clearly not accustomed to finding comfort within intimate attachments. This difficulty in being absorbed in intimate relation to her therapists kept her at a distance from the sense of security and pleasure that would have allowed for an easier reflective consideration of her trauma memory. She had talked early on in the therapeutic process about having to hold herself apart from her family, not letting them see who she really was, for fear they would destroy her. It was this honest presentation of self that was slowly becoming possible as the therapy progressed. The most poignant example of her venturing out of hiding in the group was a gift to everyone, at the end of therapy, of a most cleverly and humorously constructed crossword puzzle that captured the emotional life of the group in simple phrases that fit together in a complex matrix. To us, this was a statement in more ways than one.

Reflective appraisal of the trauma memory involves standing back and dispassionately observing the past, while at the same time being aware of the intense and overwhelming nature of emotion and meaning connected to the past. It is a state of dual consciousness that allows one to both experience and see from the outside. Alice was a scientist at heart, and by profession, and was a natural for observing and analyzing her experiences from a distance. It was the emotional connection to the traumatic material that came more slowly, in part because it required accepting the protection of a trusting attachment that she had early on in life learned to live without. Alice's course in therapy is an important illustration of the complexity of creating a context in which a survivor can in some ways forgo a lifelong adaptation and successfully communicate with emotional depth about things too painful to remember.

## Conclusions

The group of adult survivors of childhood incest whom we treated in this study were likely representative of the larger group of treatment-seeking incest survivors in some ways, and likely unrepresentative in others. We say "likely" because there is currently no definitive information about the characteristics of the population of women who were sexually abused within the context of their childhood family, even those limited to clinical samples. There really isn't any consensual information about which characteristics might be relevant to deliberations about the likely safety of, and responsiveness to, trauma-focused interventions. The criteria for subject selection we used in the current study represented our own point of view based on our knowledge of the trauma literature and our extensive clinical experience with adult female survivors of childhood incest.

Our best guess about the representativeness of our current sample is that they are more educated, more highly functioning, more motivated, and generally more resourceful than we would expect of the general norm for treatment-seeking incest survivors. On the other hand, our subjects were highly traumatized, highly symptomatic, and had long-standing adaptations in place that would challenge the most experienced of therapists. Furthermore, our sample was composed of a quite heterogeneous group of women, each of whom presented a slightly different treatment challenge. As we argued earlier in chapter 1, we would place our group of survivors as a whole, in reference to a population of trauma survivors, somewhere in the midrange of overall severity in regard to both trauma response and ease of responsiveness to treatment.

The research context of our provision of psychotherapy greatly enhanced our ability to evaluate the effectiveness of our work. Quantitative changes in symptoms and trauma themes served as useful markers of our progress and allowed us to gauge the appropriateness of the length of our intervention for the group of subjects as a whole, as well as for individual survivors. The evaluation of Complex PTSD symptoms and trauma themes proved to be invaluable in aiming a broader lens toward both our success and the areas where our interventions fall relatively short. Finally, the improvement in psychiatric symptoms not routinely associated with trauma-focused interventions convinced us further of the breadth of our effects.

Considering symptoms and themes contextualized by our more complete understanding of individual survivors provided a complementary use of our quantitative data that appreciated the uniqueness of each of our subjects. Contextualized in this way, the systematically collected information on symptoms and themes contributed to our ability to conceptualize the dynamics of traumatic adaptations, as illustrated in our case examples in this chapter. Even with the availability of a much larger treatment sample and an appropriate control group, we would still argue for a careful consideration of fully contextualized data on individual study participants.

# Chapter 4

# The Evolution of Trauma-Focused Work in Individual and Group Settings

The second half of the book deals with the actual process of the psychotherapy in much greater detail. In this first chapter, we describe how the process evolves over the course of the year in both individual and group settings. For each of the four 3-month periods, we have relied on our therapy notes, the notes of our observing students, the videotapes, and team discussions in order to represent as accurately as possible what is most salient to us about the therapeutic work. In the two chapters that follow, we will present an even closer look at the therapy sessions, with actual dialogue from the individual settings and narrative accounts of the group interactions.

## An Introduction to the Settings

As a way of introducing a more detailed description of the four quarters of our interventions, we would like to highlight the intimate ties of the work in the two settings, as well as the most distinguishing features of the work that we each do. While we do not know which aspects of our interventions, if any, are indispensable, our experience of doing the therapy was that we had a hard job to do, and to the extent that we could reinforce and complement each others' efforts, we would be that much more likely to succeed.

## The Collaboration Between Therapists

The defining nature of our collaboration in reality, and as communicated to the members of the study over time in myriad ways, was that we were working *together* to create a place of safety and growth. The women in our study knew that we had worked together for some time and that we respected and liked each other. They knew that we talked about them every week for the purpose of maximizing our potential to help them. They also came to understand that they could rely on either of us to help them, in a straightforward way, with any problem they might be having with the other, without risk of embarrassment to them or conflict for us. For example, in response to a complaint about RB not talking enough, SR might encourage the group member to talk to him about it, supporting the idea that it was safe to do so, and letting the group member know that she had the power to negotiate a comfortable relationship with him. Likewise, in response to a complaint about SR's confrontational style, RB might help a group member assert her needs. While we were strongly allied in our treatment goals, it was clear to the group members that our styles were very different and that generally we were as autonomous as we were connected. Our complementary styles led us to approach the therapeutic goals with a different emphasis.

## The Emphasis in Individual Psychotherapy:
### Creating an Ease of Communication

The individual work emphasizes bringing into focus the trauma memory by creating a dialogue that enables imaginative capacities and relies to whatever extent is necessary on metaphoric communication. As we have stressed throughout, the revivifications and adaptational transformations of the abusive experiences are difficult to recognize, but they provide compelling data to a survivor about the nature of her problems when they are thoughtfully regarded. The investigative activity that leads to an unfolding of a more integrated trauma story is greatly enhanced by a broadening of normative social conventions regarding how to communicate about one's experiences. A common language that tolerates reflection, ambiguity and complexity, playfulness, and positive regard is developed in a unique creative partnership between survivor and therapist in the individual therapy setting.

The lifting of social conventions about communication creates a freedom that nurtures a way of thinking that is less imposed upon by all the factors that clouded the possibility of knowing in one's rational mind (in the way that one knew in one's experiential mind) what had happened in childhood. A mundane example of this mode of communication comes to mind in one of our own interactions, one of many where we found some pleasure in contemplating an important ingredient of the therapy on more neutral ground. SR, out of town exploring potential opportunities for her family, was in a situation that demanded some very important decisions to be made rapidly. She called RB to check in with him about work, and he asked her where she was. She responded that she was in the Twilight Zone, consciously intending to communicate something about her anxiety, but also unselfconsciously communicating something more complex in her choice of metaphor. RB's engaging response, "What's the Twilight Zone like this time of year?" conveyed an acceptance of, and even positive regard for, the chosen form of communication, even though he would have liked to know what city she was in. His response allowed for an immediate playful connection from which they could jointly reflect on the subjective reality of SR's experience.

The lifting of social conventions about communication in the individual therapy coincides with the initial securing of the attachment between therapist and survivor during the first month of treatment. One way that the change in norms is accomplished is to establish a form of creative conversation that is clearly demarcated from normal face-to-face conversation by a structured time set aside within each session. A variety of techniques are available to allow a shift from the conventional conversational context to a less guarded, more imaginatively permissive dialogue. These techniques are drawn from a variety of disparate traditions that have in common the idea that it is possible to access, in the therapeutic context, a natural capacity for relaxed absorption in imagery-based associations that are socially engaged, but not constrained, by an attentively absorbed therapist (see, for example, Barlow & Cerny, 1988; Csikszentmihaly, 1990; Freud, 1975; Havens, 1986; Lyons & Keane, 1989; and Spiegel, 1989). The absorption on the survivor's part, it is presumed, will regularly lead to meaningful information about her adaptation. The clear structure established by the various techniques has the added benefit of providing a kind of container for the emotional intensity associated with the reflective work, a container that allows for control and privacy. Finally, working side by side an equally absorbed conversational partner makes an overwhelming task tolerable. The shift in conversational context, then, in no way sets this emphasis in individual therapy apart from the therapeutic social context we have previously described.

We do not want to give the impression that the particular kind of structuring that RB provides for the trauma work in the individual setting is either necessary or sufficient for achieving a reflective state

vided some overarching statement about the possibilities for being a powerful woman in relationship to a gentle man.

## A Community of Peers

The joining of group members in a common commitment creates a social network and a powerful *social reference* that encourages the ability to be oneself. There is an acceptance and understanding in this reference group, like in no other, of the significance of having been sexually abused within the family context. This acceptance signals a safety in "publicly" exploring the depths of one's inner experience without fear of rejection and humiliation. The understanding provides a contrast to the alienation that is usually felt in groups or dyads, an alienation that inevitably leads to a hiding of oneself from others so as not to appear different. While conformity pressures are a part of social life at all stages of development and exist in regard to people who hold different places in a hierarchy of social power, one is particularly struck by the potency of peer relations in childhood to call forth the dichotomy of being either on the inside or the outside of the only available group. The psychotherapy group offers a community of peers to which one can belong without holding back one's childhood experiences.

The creation of a social reference by the survivors' participation in a common goal not only tempers alienation but also provides a truly prideful group identification. It is the social nature of human beings that their self-esteem is tied up with the degree of positive regard they have for those groups with which they are identified, be they defined by family, professional roles, gender, or age. In gender studies, for example, it is taken for granted that, as a woman, the ability to identify positively with a valued image of womanhood has a great deal to do with one's self esteem. Similarly, to hold in mind an affiliation with a valued group of survivors of childhood incest greatly increases the likelihood of being able to take pride in one's identity. When one observes the courageous work of the members of a group of survivors such as we have studied, it is easy to imagine how being a part of the group becomes an important source of self-respect.

The strong identification as a group occurs fairly naturally and rapidly and is reinforced by the opportunity for collaboration on the therapeutic work provided by the structuring of the group dynamic. The actual time in the group is shared among brief weekly "check ins" by all group members, intensive work between SR and one or two individual group members in any particular week, and group discussions among members on issues of general concern. But involvement of all group members is encouraged at all times by the clear message that they have an important therapeutic role. With the oversight of SR, the interactions among group members provide a lesson in the power of social support that can easily be taken outside of the group setting. In our study, the members actually spent considerable time together outside of the therapeutic context, and considerable time within the group setting learning how to negotiate meaningful relationships and resolve conflicts with one another. Clearly the pleasure in peer intimacy enhanced the buffer against painful exposure to traumatic pasts. It was like having a backdrop of power and comfort in numbers against which stories of helplessness and alienation lost some of their force.

## The First 3 Months

In the first 3 months of the therapy, the negotiation by survivors of relationships with others who were part of the therapeutic settings, as well as with members of their families of origin, was a salient part of the work. The structuring of a reflective dialogue in individual therapy was also an important focus of this first quarter of the year. In the group setting, the theme work was well under way by the end of the 3-month period. Even in these early months, issues of self-definition and relation to others were paramount. The first 3 months was in many ways the hardest period of therapy because of the obvious emotional intensity of the work, the unfamiliarity of ways of coping with it, and the relative invisibility of the benefits associated with enduring the suffering.

## Negotiating Relationships for the Therapeutic Work

The group of survivors who entered our study were motivated to get right down to the work of understanding the current presence or influence of their childhood trauma, as well as its impact in the past. Since the work was to be collaborative, it was necessary to secure protective attachments with RB and SR and to strike an appropriate balance between autonomy and connection with one another. During this early phase, the group members also concentrated on their relationships with their mothers in the present perhaps as a way of coming to terms with the intuitive knowledge that their mothers were not going to be any more of a safety net now than they had been during the childhood abuse.

NEGOTIATING WITH THE THERAPISTS. In the first month of individual therapy, the major emphasis is in challenging implicit relational assumptions that the survivor brings to the interaction with the therapist. From the therapist's side, this involves both *experiencing* the pulls for a certain kind of relatedness, as well as *standing outside* and observing these pulls. It also involves establishing a dialogue around the relational assumptions brought by the survivor to treatment. As we shall illustrate, this dialogue respectfully includes the survivor in the observations, and orients her to her adaptive capacities in regard to presumed traumatic experiences. While the exact nature of traumatic experiences may be unknown, the psychotherapy assumes a trauma focus in all respects, including in the generation of hypotheses regarding styles of relating to the therapist. For the therapist, it is no small challenge, even with one foot in and one foot out, so to speak, to continually confront the fact of the survivor's abuse and not react out of an exaggerated sense of responsibility or helplessness. It is obviously harmful to promise more than is deliverable; to believe to know more than is knowable; to be empathic out of anxiety, guilt, or shame; to be an overinvolved hero who makes up for past deprivations; or, on the other side, to keep at such a distance as to avoid the overwhelming nature of the survivor's experiences, which can leave even the most experienced therapist humbled.

It took some time for our study participants to understand that we wanted to help *them* take control of their trauma work and support each other as individuals with different needs and some common ground. Initially they were often either too concerned about accommodating us in our research needs and expectations, or somewhat resistant to accepting help in anticipation of being intruded upon or controlled by the therapeutic process. For example, in Jo's case, as described earlier, there was a tendency to challenge RB about such things as the reliability of memory or the authority of the therapy profession. In making it clear that there was no demand for conformity, only a demand for mutual respect, the possibility that she would be helped to draw her own conclusions in her own time, and with whatever privacy she needed, became apparent to her. And in complaining about Jo's implied objectification of him as a member of a corrupt profession, RB encouraged Jo to take him seriously as a unique individual as well. Out of a sensitive concern not to dominate or deprive, therapists often fail to demand respect. If

RB had unquestioningly accepted Jo's symbolization of her anger with authority as a legitimate complaint toward him and his colleagues, it would have been frightening for Jo. To demand respect also sends a message about both the therapist's and the survivor's durability. Neither are so fragile as to choose entanglement over being fully present with one another. Finally, without redramatizing the survivor's traumatic adaptation in any sense, it can be examined in an empathic and respectful way. By conveying an understanding of Jo's reservations about the therapeutic contract as a natural response to past betrayals, there was an important message about her agency and worth. For example, Jo's apprehension about the therapy was also manifest in her concern about the confining nature of the physical space in the psychotherapy office. When Jo shamefully revealed that she felt like dashing for the door when RB was silent, he told her that she was doing a good job of being cautious, and that trust is something that only comes with time. RB also moved his chair out of her path to the door.

Compared to the emphasis on relational assumptions in the individual work during the first 3 months, in the group setting the relationship between SR and the group members was less of a focus. This was, due, in large part, to the difference in therapeutic setting, but also partly because of the differences in gender and style between SR and RB. The group setting was by its very nature less hierarchical, and SR's position of authority was less salient. The tone of the group was often defined by positive excitement, camaraderie, and laughter, clearly reflecting the experience of power and comfort in numbers, enhanced by an all-female presence and by SR's reliance on humor to establish an intimate workplace.

There were areas of concern, however, related to establishing a protective attachment with SR. One, as mentioned previously, was the discussion in group about concerns of individual members about their relationship with RB. These discussions not only cemented the collaborative nature of our work but also permitted a sharing of perspectives about RB among group members that enhanced their receptivity to reflect on their own implicit relationship assumptions. For example, Annie had become suspicious at one point that RB had laughed at her when she expressed vulnerability. Using the group as a "sounding board" for her concerns, she got the message that everyone would be surprised if that had in fact happened. The suggestion from the group that she raise the question with RB encouraged honesty in the relationship with RB and self-reflection on her part.

Relational assumptions did come into play at certain times regarding the expression of anxieties about the relationship with SR. In the 2nd month, for example, Alice, with RB's encouragement, described how she did not feel like herself in group because of SR's probing style, which reminded her of her intrusive mother. SR acknowledged her confrontational style and asked Alice if she could find a way to signal her if she was becoming uncomfortable, because she shared Alice's concern that she not feel retraumatized in the group by feeling powerless. She expressed her interest in together finding some way for Alice to experience greater control over the therapeutic process in the group setting. SR often initiated discussions with group members, even in the absence of any expressed anxiety, about whether there was something in her approach to the collaboration that was making them uncomfortable.

Another issue regarding SR that came up in group bore some relationship to the fact that some members of the group had often been in the role of caretaker for their mothers. Jo asked SR if she could ask her a personal question. SR said that she could, with the understanding that SR probably would not answer it since her role in the group was different from that of the members. She alone had the responsibility for continually holding their therapeutic needs in mind. Jo then asked SR if she were a survivor of childhood sexual abuse, a question for which there seemed to be a broad interest among the group members, and in which there was an implicit challenge about whether SR could "understand." In the course of conversation about why it might be important for them to know the answer to the question, several group members told stories of the role reversals in their families in regard to caretaking. They also told of previous therapists who had disclosed stories of their own abuse, only to create an insecurity about the ability of the therapist to provide protection with ease. Thus, pulls for a certain kind of relatedness carried weight at certain times in the group as well as the individual setting, and required the institution of reflectiveness on both the therapist's and group member's part.

In the work of negotiating relationships with the therapists during the first 3 months of therapy, the groundwork is being laid for a general orientation to appraise one's behavior reflectively and empathically, with the help of knowledgeable and compassionate mentors. There is also an expectation established for respectful behavior to be reciprocated by the survivor, which sets limits that enhance a sense of protection and an attitude of competency. When challenging implicit assumptions that have provided the survivor with a sense of control in the past, the therapist must begin to establish the possibility of a respectful intimate relationship to cushion the intensification of terrifying emotions associated with traumatic childhood experiences.

NEGOTIATING WITH THE GROUP MEMBERS. By the reports over the years of many group members of survivor groups similar to the one in this study, it is clear that the experience of being in the same room for the first time with other survivors has a strong emotional impact.

The bond that is formed almost immediately is based on an experiential knowledge of sharing a similar life tragedy, which evolves over time into a solid connection based as much on differentiation of experiences as on common ground. During the first quarter of the group psychotherapy, the members establish a meaningful alliance that facilitates a commitment to the group relationships over the course of the year. They come to recognize their individuality as well as their ability to build a community by their involvement in each other's work. A dream that Caroline reported having during the end of the first month of treatment illustrates how a strong group identification begins to develop early on in the therapeutic process. In the dream, a group of "women police" arrive to rescue her from a situation in which she is physically overwhelmed by a man. The women police know to come to her aid because they recognize that justice must be served. She thinks of the women police as "women heroes" and begins to imagine that she might be able to include herself as a member of this group.

To best illustrate the important therapeutic role that the group members play for each other, we are simply going to provide brief vignettes of group members interacting during the first 3 months of therapy. Although the full context of the group setting can best be appreciated in the narrative accounts of the group work in the final chapter, these vignettes allow for an appreciation of the collaboration among the survivors in the group. We hesitate at this point to offer any particular organization to the nature of the interaction among the group members, but suffice to say their responses to one another are characterized by reassurance, comforting, support, sympathizing, sharing experiences and emotions, a desire to learn from one another, and an ability to support the work of the therapists. As a therapist in this setting, it is quite remarkable to observe the thoughtful and humane interchange that evolves among the

women. The vignettes follow in list form. While the interactions described are direct representations of what transpired in the group,
sometimes interactions are grouped in ways that do not reflect the
actual sequencing of dialogue within a particular time frame.

1. Jo tells Ceci that she has had similar experiences of not always
being able to hold in mind things she remembers. She says how she,
like Ceci, also goes through periods of thinking she's crazy and
thinking that her uncle (suspected perpetrator) is a good person.
She encourages Ceci about her plan to reread old journal entries,
saying that the same thing has been helpful to her, Jo.

2. Annie describes how it is difficult for her to be intimate in relationships. Jesse says that she was accused of the same thing in her
marriage but that she was not aware of keeping a distance. She asks
Annie about her own level of awareness while in a relationship. She
is looking to Annie for information to gain insight into her own situation. Later in the same group, Annie describes her worries about
her adolescent daughter's desire to be sexually intimate. Jesse com-
ments on how they must have an amazingly good relationship for
her daughter to talk to her about it. Other group members chime in,
in agreement.

3. Jo talks about reading a symptom checklist in a book, seeing
how depressed and angry she is, and wondering whether this is how
she will always be. Caroline says that she has seen the same list but
that she can honestly say she doesn't have all those symptoms anymore. She talks about how when she directed anger to the appropriate targets, she ceased to get angry inappropriately. In the same
session, in response to a similar worry expressed by Annie about
whether she would ever be better, Caroline tells of an ad for an
abused-children's clinic whose slogan is, "We teach them to walk

with the abuse, not to be led by it." Caroline then describes what healing from the abuse is like for her.

4. Ceci says that she would like to have her boyfriend come with her to her session with RB because she feels too much shame to allow RB to comfort her if she becomes really upset. Caroline describes how having a male therapist made her realize that she'd never been emotionally involved with a man without being sexually involved as well.

5. Jesse talks about telling her academic adviser about the incest, describing her mixed feelings about having said anything. Caroline tells how she told her fellow students that she was a survivor of childhood sexual abuse in order to challenge their assumption that "it doesn't happen in nice, normal-appearing families." Ceci tells how she "shut someone up" at church who was talking about the false memory syndrome by letting them know that she was just now dealing with memories of childhood sexual abuse herself.

6. Jesse describes how difficult the group was for her at the beginning because she remembered everything that happened to her, unlike the other members. Jo and Caroline respond that Jesse's way of differentiating herself early on made them angry, uncomfortable, and insecure. Jesse goes on to say that she chose to forget the emotions rather than the events. The following week, Alice talks about how difficult it is for her to be herself and reveal what she is feeling when she is in group. Caroline offers that she has noticed how different Alice is in other settings, more at ease. She says to Alice that it must be frustrating for her to know herself but be unable to be that way. A week later, Annie talks about how when she first came to group, she felt like a "hillbilly" in contrast to everyone else but that after she talked, she felt a connection with the others because

*Naming the Shadows*

they understood her experience. She goes on to say how she had felt so out of place because everyone else was so successful and had gone to school, whereas she couldn't even sit in class without having a panic attack. Caroline responds that she had panic attacks in school, too. Ceci says, "But you're a welder. That's the coolest thing in the world!" In the same group, Caroline describes how guilty she has felt all week because she had asked to have time this week in group. Jo responds that the reason she came to group tonight, even though she didn't want to, was that she wanted to listen to what Caroline had to say, out of a commitment to her.

7. Jesse talks about a dream she describes as bizarre, where she was on an archeological dig and was captured by "aborigines." She pretended to be pregnant because then they would keep her alive. Both she and her estranged husband were captive in the dream, tied to child swings. She says, "I had to fake it to survive." Group members comment on how the dream might express what it was like for her growing up. Ceci, for example, notes how Jesse would talk about being her father's (perpetrator) favorite, and how she got special treatment from him because she was a female. She also says that perhaps Jesse feels bound to her childhood in a way that keeps her from fully living out her life in the present.

8. Jo says she was impressed with the way Ceci off-handedly referred, in the previous group, to being sexually assaulted in high school because she has had similar experiences. She tells of how, at first, she thought about Ceci's experiences in a way to convince herself that she, Jo, wasn't abused as a child, and that her teenage experiences had caused all the problems. But then Ceci's disclosure caused her to reflect more thoughtfully on what had happened to her as a teenager. Jo tells of two assaults she experienced in high school and college. She seems, for the first time, to have some ap-

preciation of the impact they had on her. She ends by thanking Ceci for sharing her experiences, since it helped her so much to rethink her own.

9. Alice talks about her mother, describing her as passive, vulnerable, and generally inept. She talks, for example, about finding out from her brother that it was something she, Alice, said that caused her mother to attempt suicide. She tells of her mother's description of finding her, Alice, as a 4-year-old in an alley, apparently having just been molested. Evidently her mother had forgotten about the attack and only thought of it in response to Alice's asking if anything bad had ever happened to her. She explains how she does not want to tell her mother about being in the group and about going through the individual therapy process. Alice's disclosures generate lively discussion among group members. The following dialogue is in response to aspects of how Alice has presented her mother:

*Jesse:* Are you at peace now with not telling your mom about this (therapy)?

*Jo:* I want to encourage you. I was like that with my mom for four years, but she's got a lot of stuff she could tell you.

*Ceci:* My mom won't tell me anything, so I gauge by her reactions. The more nervous she gets, the closer to the truth I am.

*Caroline:* That's how I am with my mom. I start asking about good memories, then move on.

*Jo:* Aren't you pissed off at her? We're adults now. We are, they are. And we all have a responsibility to act like adults. She could help you now emotionally and she's bailing out. Doesn't that piss you off?

*Jesse:* She's so vague. Her accounts keep changing. It makes it hard for you to react.

*Ceci:* You don't have to excuse your mother.

NEGOTIATING WITH THE FAMILIES OF ORIGIN. During the first 3 months of therapy, there was a salient focus in the group setting on the members' relationships with their mothers. It seemed clear that doing the trauma work involved a consideration of the implications for relationships with mothers in the present, consideration of mothers' roles in the abusive family circumstances of their childhood, and mothers' general supportiveness in the past. As early as the 2nd week of group treatment, the discussion centered around how to cope with the complex set of feelings the group members experienced toward their mothers. Although the mothers were presented as lacking compassion and being generally dismissive and critical, they were also described as demanding a close presence in a psychological sense, which created guilt and confusion. The value in achieving some perspective on their mothers' behavior was clear and was enhanced by the members' ability to observe each other in the group setting. Whereas anger toward their mothers was intensely experienced by some, there was also a forgivingness "waiting to happen" for most, if only the mothers would support them now in their work at being themselves. What was at stake in understanding their mothers was a freedom to come to value themselves in the context of new relationships.

For the most part, the mothers of this particular group of survivors seemed incapable of joining in the therapeutic endeavor in any supportive way. On the contrary, interactions with their mothers typically led survivors to self-doubt and confusion, replicating the experience of lack of protection that apparently characterized earlier family life. As was described previously, lack of protection defines a social context that sustains a lie about the abusive nature of incest. It sustains a point of view that would be inconsistent with that of a compassionate outsider. It defines a social context that is in sharp contrast to one the survivors longed for, one that provided a mother's acceptance and support. The mothers of the women in our study seemed neither compassionate nor strong, and often seemed to have some stake in maintaining the status quo. The thoughtfulness on the part of the survivors about how to address their therapeutic work with their mothers was not matched by thoughtfulness on the other side. We remember a poignant story told by Jo during the 2nd month of treatment about how her mother had strategically placed a *Newsweek* article regarding "false memories" in her old bedroom when she was visiting her parents' home on a weekend trip.

During the first quarter of treatment, what was perhaps most painful for the survivors in dealing with the confusion surrounding their relationships with their mothers was the growing realization of what they might stand to lose in the way of family connection. By letting go of any sense of responsibility for their mothers' disrespectful stance toward them, and by sticking to their commitment to take a new look at their childhood with more perspective and balance, there was the likelihood of a painful crumbling of illusions that sustained a sense of belonging to a family. One starts to appreciate, in listening to survivors struggling with family loyalties, how powerful the ties to their mothers actually are.

## Structuring a Reflective Dialogue

At its simplest level, the structuring of a reflective dialogue involves a combination of focused relaxation and absorption in a "central focus" or "workplace." While the nature of the workplace differs from person to person, there is in common a reliance on the survivor's ability to access a state of calm reflection with the help of a counting ritual. In this state of reflection, there is an ease of freely following cognitive and affective associations and, at the same time, an enhanced ability to sustain an observational state that counters the overwhelming pull of states of terror. The counting ritual simply involves a series of suggestions, introduced rhythmically, to focus attention, to collect oneself, to follow associations, and to observe and report on the ensuing process. As one freely enters a workplace, there is an understanding that one has the power to exit this state with a similar ritual. The ritual, of course, involves a therapist-survivor collaboration, thus holding the therapeutic relationship in mind, as well as the sense of structure and control. The challenges to securing this reflective state relate to overriding the posttraumatic states of mind that demand hypervigilance or distraction.

At a more complex level, the structuring of a reflective dialogue inspires confidence in the possibility of moving imaginatively into the trauma work from a place of safe grounding in the present. As the relationship between survivor and therapist develops an identity that sets it apart from relationships associated with the traumatic experiences, the ease of controlling revivifications and separating the present from the past is enhanced. Likewise, metaphoric reminders of experiences that evoke a sense of relief from traumatic states of mind may be developed during this structuring period to provide a familiar entry to a more secure state of mind. In general, the provision of protection in the therapeutic context through *controlled* exposure to traumatic material, a positive absorption in the therapeutic attachment, and an emphasis on the separation of present and past is the important and salient backdrop against which the structuring occurs.

At this more complex level, the structuring of a reflective dialogue takes on a more individualistic character that grows out of the particular nature of the relationship between survivor and therapist, and depends on what survivors creatively recruit for their own sense of comfort. In Jesse's case, for example, RB initially focused on constructing a history that would identify Jesse's natural ability to access states of positive absorption. She initially described the flow of music while playing her violin as a child, and how she could get lost for hours sketching an *imagined* self that could say and do what in reality she could not. As there developed a growing alliance with her helpers in the first couple of months of therapy, her associations led her to recall the "gentle and fun" environment of her grandparents' house where she was raised as a young child. She remembered a warm, bustling kitchen, filled with friendly conversation and delicate aromas, where attachments were not yet complicated by her parents' betrayal. Her grandparents' kitchen provided a starkly contrasting image to her parents' kitchen, where she vividly recalled being beaten for eating too slowly. It is as if sustaining pleasant associations from the present and the past are allied in providing a lens through which to view a traumatic past.

We have observed in general that a place of comfort in imagination paradoxically reveals the traumatic imprint, even as it is now encased in a number of protective layers. In at least some cases, it seems clear that the place of comfort bears a direct relationship to the traumatic adaptation. Annie, for example, had been able with RB's help to transform, during initial structuring efforts, an experience of tension and tightness in her body that she described as being like a hopelessly tangled yarn. With RB's suggestion that she could imaginatively turn the yarn into whatever she wanted, she talked about a yarn blanket that brought a sense of protection, and about an image of a flying cape that evoked a feeling of power and freedom and the sense of being above it all. At the same time that there was great comfort in this imagery, it also opened the way to associations that addressed the deep humiliation she had experienced at the hands of her abusers. Likewise, Jo's comforting metaphor evolved as an imagined hawk soaring above a mountain, inspiring a sense of being strong, free, and uplifted. The link to associated revivifications of disturbing elements of her uncle's threatening presence became clear as she described some weeks later an experience at age 7 or 8 of standing at the railing on the second floor of a mall, imagining jumping off, wishing to fly. In other cases like Ceci's, described previously in chapter 1, what unfolded over time was that the comforting, protected, sunlit apartment had the same unusual triangular shape as her grandfather's attic, but nevertheless seemed to provide a sense of safety because of the recognition that danger no longer existed in the present day. Whether her artistic transformation of the dreaded attic into a sunlit haven more generally reflected her adaptation to her traumatic childhood experiences is certainly an intriguing question.

The structuring of a reflective dialogue is a way into the trauma work that precludes drowning in it, getting lost in it, or otherwise disappearing in a retraumatizing way. While we have provided our observations about how the process of controlled, emotionally absorbing exposure to traumatic material begins with this structuring, we certainly do not have all the answers to important conceptual questions about this process. We remain somewhat in awe of the complexity, artistry, and logic of human adaptational processes. As we observed Jesse, Annie, Jo, Ceci, Caroline, and Alice make their way toward an understanding of the persistent presence of their traumatic childhood experiences, we experienced a growing respect for their ability to join their own resourcefulness with our support and guidance. Each survivor, in her own style, was able to open a door to an extraordinary network of associations that revealed over time the enduring emotional significance of incestuous relationships in her early family life.

## Confronting Trauma Themes

At the core of sexual trauma is the experience of not being in control of one's sexuality and having one's physical and psychological boundaries violated. For a child to accept her helplessness in being sexually traumatized would be like acknowledging an obliteration of her agency and confronting the threat of loss of a sense of self. To accept her helplessness in being traumatized might often involve a recognition of random and meaningless danger in the world, or the power of trusted others to betray and exploit. Thus it is not surprising that survivors blame themselves for their abuse as a way of maintaining an illusion of control. But this illusion can sustain feelings of guilt and shame, a sense of being flawed or damaged and unworthy of love, an inability to master feelings of rage or fear, and a distorted understanding of the potential for danger and betrayal, all of which may dangerously drive behavior over the course of development. Helping survivors confront the traumatic meanings that surround their exposure to incest can involve profound grief for them, in the loss of their illusions and in the understanding of their tragedies. But it also offers the truth in assigning blame and a new perspective on one's courage and the possibilities for a rewarding life.

The theme of self-blame was very salient during group sessions in the first three months of treatment. Survivors experienced responsibility for a range of things including the persistence of abuse over time in childhood, the failure to protect siblings from an abusive family environment, the suffering of their mothers during their childhood, and the exploitative treatment they endured as adults at the hands of men. In this particular group of survivors, the discussions of blame often carried an intellectual awareness of the irrationality of taking responsibility for things over which one has no power. It was relatively easy for survivors to object when *other members* blamed themselves for the malevolence or lack of responsibility of adults in their family, or for the disrespectful or abusive behavior of peers. But, when considering their own childhood family situations, or their close relationships as adults, there was often a blind spot and a resistance to accepting the straightforward message that they should not take responsibility for others' abusiveness in any way. To make successful interventions around the issue of blame, it was essential to convey an understanding of how a survivor constructed her role of responsibility in her family, to be listening for current instances of that point of view in the present, and to move back and forth between present and past, sawing away at the hold of the past by trying to show the value of letting go of this sense of responsibility in the present.

Jesse spoke about self-blame in a number of different contexts during this period of group treatment. She held herself responsible for not putting a stop to the sexual abuse by her father, which began at age 12 and continued until she left for college. She described her sexual relationship with her father as including an element of choice on her part, and as being driven by a pragmatism that was largely financial. Without any acknowledgment of the emotional urgency of family ties for her, she said that she simply struck a bargain with her father, in her own mind, that she would not disturb the order of things in the family in return for financial support.

Along with this numbing of emotional awareness about her lack of power and control in her pathological family home, there was an understanding at the outset of treatment that she was preoccupied at times by rage toward her parents and her estranged husband. And along with her assertion that justice had been served to her father by her estrangement from him in the present, there was a persistent desire to set the family record straight about what had happened, and her yearning to achieve a sense of belonging in her parents' home.

As we noted in chapter 2, Jesse was often confused about whether her anger toward her estranged husband was justified. She would go back and forth between being angry at her husband for his insults and other disrespectful behavior toward her and feeling allied with his way of relating to her to the point of feeling shameful.

This dynamic spread to interactions with men in her work environment as well, which she described in some detail in the first several months of group therapy. For example, Jesse described her disgust at a much older supervisor at work for asking her out on a date. At the same time that she expressed anger at his inappropriate behavior, she also seemed to blame herself for bringing on his advances. This vacillation between anger at others for making her life so difficult on the one hand, and acceptance of blame for difficult experiences on the other, even spread to the way she conceptualized her inability to achieve what she would have liked to earlier on in her studies. For the most part, she blamed herself for her lack of achievements and her lack of satisfying relationships.

There were obvious parallels between how Jesse had coped with her father's betrayal in holding herself responsible while at the same time harboring an intense anger toward him for the incest, and how she experienced herself in all spheres of her life. The inextricable relationships among self-blame and the other trauma themes, and their potential for describing a persistent dynamic for Jesse, were visible early on in the group work. The therapeutic challenge was to try to allow Jesse to understand the meaning of her childhood coping attempts in descriptive thematic terms, to reconstruct her childhood experience with an adult perspective in the therapeutic context, and to see how the original construction of her childhood trauma continued to define her present world in maladaptive ways. These goals were accomplished by putting the observable thematic data in front of her in as persistent a way as possible. By feeding back to her what she would repetitively say, by drawing thematic parallels to her relationship with her father, and by asking her to consider the evidence for thematic interpretations, the opportunity was there for her to reconstruct her understanding of the incest and modulate the intense emotions that followed.

To move toward a conceptualization of recovery in the language of trauma themes keeps the therapeutic dialogue close to a survivor's actual experience, since the trauma themes were derived from the voices of survivors. While the importance of a particular theme will vary across survivors and across time, and while the dynamic interplay of themes can take many forms, the salience of the theme of self-blame was unquestionable. In recognizing the therapeutic importance of truth in assigning blame in Jesse's case, we believe that had this truth been offered at the time of the incest by a protective adult, and had responsibility for the repercussions been taken out of Jesse's hands, it would have profoundly affected her ability to limit her rage and her expectation of betrayal and made her more hopeful about the possibility of belonging.

## Conclusion

The survivors' orientation to appraise their behavior reflectively and empathically with the help of knowledgeable and compassionate mentors is well established during the first 3 months of the psychotherapy. Whether in communicating about the traumatic experience within the structure of the imaginative dialogue in individual therapy, or the language of trauma themes in the group context, what is being established is the survivor's ability to *observe* herself in the service of understanding the life-altering implications of her experience with childhood incest. For a survivor, the ability to evaluate how she feels about something, or to understand the motivations behind her behavior, or to consider what values are important to her, or to trust her choices are among the countless benefits that come with self-knowledge.

During this phase of psychotherapy, the survivors in our study gained confidence that the previously overwhelming intensity of the traumatic material could be approached and mastered. At the same time, the therapeutic process was frightening for survivors at times, and the approach to traumatic material was naturally punctuated with periods of rest, a kind of pacing that was strongly encouraged by us. By the end of the first quarter of therapy, the members of our study were deeply involved in the therapeutic work and had embraced a process that would allow them to move steadily toward reaping the full benefits of their hard work.

## Months 4 Through 6

The community created in the group setting intensifies in purpose as reflections on historical material and its impact in the present become more routine in the individual therapy context. In the second quarter, the negotiation of relationships among group members moves toward a new complexity that incorporates conflict. The recognition that attachments can weather differences, that not all disappointments involve betrayal, and that conflict can be resolved by conversation, derive in part from the therapist-supervised group interactions. The general untangling of an unresolved past from constructions of experiences in the present facilitate the formation on the part of survivors of more complex images of themselves and others that include both positive and negative qualities. The discovery and tolerance of gray areas and middle grounds in regard to developing relationships with peers leads to greater ease in giving and accepting support. The reactions of group members to one anothers' work continues to be genuinely supportive, and provides, alongside the individual work, an experiential understanding that the trauma work does not have to be done alone.

In our experience, developing the ability to resolve interpersonal conflict is challenging because of the very nature of the interpersonal dynamics in a situation of extreme maltreatment. If somebody you love does something to you repeatedly that you experience as abominable, it is not unreasonable to think in extreme terms, unable to incorporate another's *abusive* behavior into an image of a loving relationship in the way one might incorporate someone's annoying habits, or even someone's unintentionally hurtful transgressions. It is in fact quite reasonable, in this situation, to terminate a relationship. A child in an abusive home is, of course, in no position to do this, which often leads to an idealization of the childhood perpetrator and an intolerance for others' as well as one's own shortcomings as an adult. Conflict in a relationship can signal an intolerable kind of ambiguity that derives from the truly intolerable coexistence of love and abuse in important childhood attachments.

The group relationships evolve alongside the survivors' changing relationships with members of their family of origin, which continues to be a topic of frequent conversation in the second quarter. Family relationships, including those with mothers, siblings, and perpetrators, are now interpreted in the context of a developing new historical perspective, which reflects one of the fundamental achievements of both the individual and group work. The hard work applied toward understanding the behavior of family members is meaningful, although it often highlights the impossibility of bringing any sense of order to chaos, even with the benefit of hindsight. Survivors' attempts to renegotiate familial relationships often provide additional compelling information to add to their store of knowledge, but these efforts typically lead to a further distancing from family members rather than to a reinvestment in family bonds. While the grief associated with these interactions can be intense, the growing sense of autonomy on the part of the survivors in our study, as we approached the 6-month point in treatment, changed the balance of power in their families and provided for the possibility of real choices being made about any continuing involvement.

In the second quarter of treatment in the group setting, the emphasis on confronting trauma meanings continues and is facilitated by the immersion in trauma material in the individual setting. Anger is a prominent theme in the group during this period, and the complexity of the emotion becomes clear as survivors describe how they are frightened by it, ambivalent about it, or just plain sick of it. We believe anger can also be empowering when it is modulated because it lends an emotional legitimacy to the reality of abuse. The sense of empowerment in the members of our study is clearly evident by the 6-month point, resulting from the accumulation of self-knowledge and the firm experience of being taken seriously, which characterizes the individual work.

In the individual therapy context, the structure of the reflective dialogue continues to encourage a self-reflective state of mind and the building of a network of associations that lead to meaningful conclusions about one's behavior and history. Experiences that were unrelated, like the unset pieces of a puzzle, begin to fit together in an overarching context that has a familiar ring. The creativity involved in the therapeutic work and shared between survivor and individual therapist leads to a sense of being respectfully understood, in all of one's complexity, by another. This results in greater empathy of the survivor toward herself and is an inspiration for the work that begins to overshadow the fear that was prominent in the first 3 months. The benefits associated with an emerging sense of self become clear to survivors during this second quarter of the psychotherapeutic work.

The trauma-related experiences of being blinded by avoidance, or being overwhelmed by hypervigilant attention that precludes a solid perspective on what's important, or being terrorized by a feeling of nonexistence, are opposed by the reflective state of mind with its lifeline into the present, its tie to mastery, and its association with a secure attachment to RB. While the therapeutic work remains very emotionally challenging in the second quarter, the familiar structuring ritual works to tie the approach to traumatic material to that particular context, and to limit the experience of terrifying emotions outside of that context. As traumatic memories become more contained, there is often access, in individual therapy, to positive childhood experiences that sustained survivors through very difficult times, and there is often a new determination to locate sustaining attachments in the present. Because positive and negative experiences can comfortably coexist in the individual and the group setting, the readiness to negotiate the interpersonal world *in the present* coincides with the productive mourning of both deprivations and unrealistic ideals from the past. An example from Jo's work is illustrative of the psychotherapeutic process in the second quarter of treatment.

The coexistence of love and abuse in Jo's relationship with her uncle became a central focus for her as she began to gain historical perspective and to disentangle the imprint of the past from her current therapeutic relationships. For example, as she recalled the summers of her childhood when she would hear the screen door slam and sense herself alone with her uncle, she recognized the same fear that she had experienced being alone with RB in his office. Her unusual attentiveness to, and annoyance at, the 3:15 Carolinian—Amtrak's passenger service from Durham to Charlotte, which passed outside RB's window during their session—took on new meaning as she remembered the confusing excitement of her uncle's summertime presents. He brought her souvenirs from his job at Amtrak, which made her feel special, but which she now saw as bribes. As the complexity of her feelings began to surface and the therapeutic alliance became more secure, she and RB began to joke about the train. Its power to distract and unnerve her lessened one day after he noted that he thought he saw an older man in an Amtrak uniform desperately running away from town with the train close behind him.

RB and Jo continued over a period of weeks to enjoy their partnership in revisiting the symbolism surrounding the Durham train. An earlier dream began to make more sense. In the dream, Jo is next door with her great grandmother, the matriarchal symbol of family loyalty, when there is a collision of trains behind her house. This house is the original ancestral home, where great grandmother lived with Jo's grandparents, and where Jo's uncle would stay on his summer visits. It is the house where she had recently had the intrusive terror from a child's perspective of her uncle's threatening presence. Jo struggled with the impossible mix of remembered fondness and attachment to her uncle on the one hand, and the fear and sense of betrayal on the other. Her conflict with another group member around this time brought to the fore her long-standing questions of what is forgivable in relationships.

At the beginning of the 5th month of treatment, Jo told the group about what she called "slides" of scenes that she had seen during her individual therapy, including the secretive Amtrak gifts from her uncle, which he would leave on her nightstand, and an image of her head thrown back against a cedar headboard. She remembered not being able to breathe or call out to her mother, and the terrifying sense of her uncle's presence. While the "slides" were all disturbing, perhaps the story she told about the black widow spider, mentioned earlier, best encapsulated what she had carried with her over the years since her childhood as background for her terror. The story is worth repeating: It was the end of the workday, and she was going to go fishing with her grandmother. She picked up an old, rusty tin can to use for worms, and when she put her hand in it, there was a black widow spider. Her uncle swatted the spider from her hand with his hand and killed it. Her mother did nothing. She remembered think-ing as a child that her uncle had saved her life. She said she thought he loved her more than her parents did.

Jo's confusion about her love and dread of her uncle, her discom-fort with her father's pornography and her mother's disregard of her, her anxious and shameful feelings within her adult sexual experi-ence, and the need to reconcile her rage and her wish to be forgiv-ing, began to come together in an impressionistic big picture during the second quarter of therapy. After 6 months of treatment, she was gaining strength, and the change was illustrated by her recounting of a vivid recollection of an old oak in front of her grandparents' home. The oak conveyed a specialness that she associated with her grandmother, a strong woman who listened and took time with her. Carefree, playful moments with other children were recalled within the shade of the tree. While prior imaginative structures associated strength and freedom with a soaring hawk, the metaphor of the oak evoked a strength that was rooted in connection. While the soaring hawk was a reminder of a safety only imaginable in death, the oak was a reminder of important prior attachments and a symbol, we as-sume, of a hopefulness about trustworthy attachments in the here and now.

## The Third and Fourth Quarters

In the last 6 months of treatment, there is, in effect, a repetition of the now-familiar regimen of the therapeutic context, with a progres-sion of two steps forward, one step back, in a kind of forward-mov-ing spiral. The progression is toward a solidification of renewed potential for satisfying work and relationships and a fuller sense of meaning to life. The persistent emotional challenges associated with the trauma work preempt a straightforward motion, although heading back in the right direction after losing ground becomes easier and easier with practice. As survivors move toward the separations signaled by the completion of treatment, they are helped to reach a point of confidence that they can sustain their treatment gains, not just in the area of symptom reduction, but more important, in an internalized vision of self that is both more interpersonally connected and more solidly autonomous.

Alongside the continuity with work described for the first 6 months, in the last half of treatment there is an increasing openness to securing relationships in the present, and a decreasing preoccupation with the dangers associated with the past. As historical material comes into clearer focus, and relationships with family members become less confusing, we find survivors standing up taller, in their own shoes, trying to realistically evaluate how to relate meaningfully to the social world. In this last phase, the conclusion of therapy is experienced, for the most part, as just around the corner, and the final task of leaving a supportive environment calls forth the full use of one's resources in a difficult effort.

## Bringing Historical Material into Clearer Focus

A gradual shift in our understanding of the full extent of maltreatment in the childhood environments of our study members corresponded to their own ability to assign new meaning to what they remembered about their family life. It was, for example, only during the second half of treatment that the extent of physical as well as sexual abuse endured by our group members became clear to us. With the newly acquired perspective in the therapeutic settings, survivors were able to report and appropriately label the abusive behavior of those adults who were responsible for their care. We observed numerous instances where survivors had clearly taken their seat in the audience, so to speak, to observe their childhood family lives at some distance and to appropriately contextualize for the first time what they had experienced.

This ability to see the big picture and to scrutinize family traditions by holding them up to the public eye was associated with a parallel awareness of self and relational schemata that derived from the abusive circumstances of their childhood family life. As survivors began to appreciate just how much their adaptation over the years had influenced their experience of themselves and their expectations in relationships, they gained a certain freedom in constructing more complex images of the social world. These constructions drew from a broader sampling of life experiences, including those in the therapeutic context, and were more inclusive of their full potential to create positive outcomes in both casual and intimate social interchange. These constructions rested on a layer of optimism that was fed from pride in their growing understanding that they had indeed survived.

To have survived life in an incestuous home is to be aware that others can be dangerous, capable of betrayal and exploitation, and generally untrustworthy. As old and new relationships are evaluated and reevaluated in the context of the therapeutic work, it is a huge task to establish, on both a rational and an experiential level, some way of judging the wisdom of a particular involvement. This task dominates the work from a variety of different angles during the second half of treatment.

## Reevaluating Relationships with Family Members

In their reevaluations of relationships with family members, survivors were often aided by a feedback loop whereby experiences with their family in the present were viewed alongside memories of their family from the past. The availability of these two sets of data enhanced confidence in their evolving understanding of their family members' behavior and its impact. Sorting through these parallel data sets was emotionally intense and objectively difficult, but by the second half of treatment, survivors' observational skills were firmly in place, and they trusted that they could rely on the social group defined by the treatment effort for support, guidance, and as a source of comparison. Examples of Jo's and Ceci's work are illustrative of how family relationships were reevaluated during this phase of treatment.

There were periods, during the third quarter of treatment, when Jo's growing awareness of maltreatment in her family home revived childhood feelings of rage and despair. Even her ability to trust her therapists and other group members was shaken at times, as she struggled to understand the abuse perpetrated against her, and the inability of her parents to care for her. At the same time that Jo was intensely absorbed in reflecting on historical material, she was committed to an ongoing relationship with her mother. Visits to her family's home would remind her of childhood insults, which in turn would color her interpretation of her mother's behavior in the present.

Both in dreams reminiscent of her childhood and in her mother's reactions to her work in therapy, Jo experienced her mother's lack of sympathy for her suffering. As a result of an important series of interactions around a family reunion that was taking place at her parents' home, Jo began to be more confident about her mother's limitations, and more capable of realistic expectations for their relationship. Jo's mother had been angry at her for not wanting to attend the reunion, even though her mother was aware of how immersed she was in the painful feelings associated with family ties. This made her more confident about her belief that her mother had been unprotective of her as a child. She recalled hiding for hours in the linen closet as a child, awaiting her parents' return for lunch. Instead of being asked why she was so frightened, her mother scolded Jo for having wasted her time looking for her.

In trying to persuade Jo to go to the reunion, apparently for the sake of the appearance of family unity, she reassured Jo that her uncle would not be attending the reunion. Jo subsequently found out that her mother had lied about her uncle, and that both her parents had comfortably socialized with her uncle during the gathering. While Jo had been able to maintain her position of not going to the reunion, her sense of betrayal was nevertheless intense, and it took some time for her to regain her faith that she could receive comfort from anyone at all. The sense of community she felt from the group was critical to her regaining her footing, as she continued to try to renegotiate her relationship with her mother from a position of greater and greater strength. Both her success in holding on to herself, and her lack of success in changing her mother's ways, were illustrated in the final month of treatment, when she was able to joke about putting her family up for sale.

Ceci's experience of her family members' failure to protect her was similar to Jo's. Around the middle of treatment, Ceci's investigative talents had been focused for a time on a thoughtfully planned trip to visit her grandparents' home and to reacquaint herself with her mother's younger sisters. An abundance of evidence began to surface regarding the abusiveness of Ceci's grandfather, and this evidence was in stark contrast to the view, vehemently held by both Ceci's grandmother and her mother, of her grandfather as an easygoing, family man. During the third quarter of treatment, Ceci's interactions with her parents around the focus of her therapeutic efforts led to the realization that they would not stand by her in her insistence that the truth be told.

Ceci's fear of betrayal at this point in treatment seemed clearly tied to her profound disappointment in her parents' lack of compassion for her. She believed that her parents cared more about preserving false appearances of a normal family life than they did about what had happened to her as a child. While she had no desire to do anything hurtful, she realized that she would have to firmly assert her rights to privacy and autonomy in order to undermine the power of her parents to confuse her. They continued to demand loyalty to the family at all cost, and resented her distance. They told other members of the family, by way of explaining Ceci's attempts to have the family face itself, that she was mentally ill. Ceci's brothers were allied with her parents. It was a painful challenge for her to hold on to what she knew to be true without any validation from the nuclear family she had had to depend on as a child.

The members of our study found more support in the treatment context for their efforts to maintain integrity in relationships than they could garner from their parents and siblings. In the case of all the survivors, it was necessary to achieve a clear independence of perspective from that of the members of their childhood family home, even though the degree of contact maintained with nuclear family members varied from survivor to survivor. Perhaps because of the resourcefulness of the survivors we studied, they remained hopeful about fostering families of their own with a commitment to kindness and care.

## A New Sense of Self in Relationships

During the last half of treatment, Ceci maintained a growing confidence in her ability to see for herself, without her parents' validation, what had been the true nature of her childhood family life. As she attempted to change the underlying assumptions and rules of her relationship with her family, she was clear about needing to take a strong stand about her point of view. Her character and strength during this process of negotiation with her parents were admirable and represented some of what she could carry with her as the therapy came to a close. A dream of Ceci's during the third quarter of work is illustrative. In the dream, Ceci goes to a doctor because there is a hair in her eye. The doctor tells her that it is nothing and that she should just ignore it. After she persists in her complaints of discomfort, he agrees to remove it. To his surprise as he is pulling it out, he discovers that the hair extends quite far inside. The doctor remarks that he does not know how she could have lived with it for so long.

For all the survivors in our study, the ability to see things more clearly in general was enhanced by the trauma-focused work undertaken during the therapy. For each survivor, a more independent sense of self, unencumbered by the force of the traumatic imprint, emerged in the second 6-month period. This sense of self carried with it a new confidence in evaluating ongoing intimate peer involvement, as well as potential new alliances. There was a new facility in applying one's analytic skills to processing information and organizing experience in regard to one's interpersonal life. Equally important, there was a new facility in applying one's *intuitive* skills in making judgments about the trustworthiness of individual relationships. As we discussed in chapter 1 (see reference to Epstein, 1994), it is the intuitive or experiential system that produces information often more compelling and more likely to influence behavior.

During the second half of treatment, the members of our study were becoming familiar with the intuitive wisdom that results from the interaction of rational and experiential ways of knowing, which was a great source of pride and satisfaction. The intuitive wisdom was also a source of safety, as survivors became more consistently able to discriminate potentially dangerous from potentially rewarding relationships. There was a running joke in the group about "creep blindness" and "creep radar." These terms coined by RB so captured the members' experiences of the changes in therapy that it was as if once you had "creep radar," you had it made.

While it is true that new ways of relating left the drive of one's traumatic past behind, it is also true that being a survivor of childhood incest remained an important part of the identity of the women in our study. It was a salient issue for many of the women even in casual social interchange. There were discussions, for example, about who to tell, under what circumstances, and what to expect in the way of reactions. It was a struggle, about not having to hide or limit the possibilities for finding common ground and social support on the one hand, and being able to define the boundaries of needed privacy and protection from vulnerability on the other. It was also a matter of integrity, in the sense of commitment to not turning one's back on the knowledge of what cruelty human beings can inflict on one another. For many of the survivors in our study, facilitating a broader social awareness about child abuse gave their life greater meaning. The safety of future generations of children was firmly on their minds.

## Bringing the Work to a Close

The difficulty separating from the therapeutic context provided a final and important opportunity to resist old ways of adapting to painful interpersonal circumstances and to practice new ways of securing lasting attachments. The challenge for our study members was to see their way clear to tolerating the separation from therapy, without in any way undermining or relinquishing the meaningful connections that had been established over the course of the year. For example, in the last quarter of therapy, both Ceci and Jesse began creating distance between themselves and the therapeutic community as a way of dealing with loss, each in her own distinctive style. The task from the therapists' side was to help survivors maintain a meaningful continuity with their past through their nurturant relationships with us and the members of the group.

When we initially started the study, we were somewhat apprehensive about the unnatural 1-year time limit imposed on the therapeutic work. It became clear to us over time, however, that this time limit was consistent with what we were trying to accomplish in the way of fostering autonomy and agency among the members of our study. We were not, of course, insisting that by the end of a year, everyone should be able to continue to engage the therapeutic process, as needed, without the strong support we had provided. We were, on the other hand, convinced of the importance of asserting our confidence in the strength and resourcefulness we had observed, and of echoing our members' excitement and pride about their progress and the prospect of life without "treatment." The imposed time limit actually represented an informed estimation, on our part, of how to best mark our expectations about the readiness to move on from a firmly established home base.

## Conclusions

The model of being both allied and separate in relationships was evident in our therapeutic efforts over the course of the year in a number of ways. It was illustrated in the collaboration between us that was observed by the members of our study. It was highlighted by the way we self-consciously defined the therapeutic context of allowing autonomy and providing protection to survivors, and by the way we limited the protection by the ending of the study. It was experienced by survivors in the establishment of common ground and differentiation among themselves in the context of the group.

In helping survivors toward a new way of approaching casual and intimate relationships, the respect we conveyed for the complexity involved in *putting themselves forward* in the course of the trauma work was central. Over the course of the year, the openness to new experiences and the freedom to value themselves in relationships was gained through self-knowledge painfully derived from reflection on the lingering impact of historical material. Likewise, the skill in processing and organizing experiences both analytically and intuitively was gained through this accumulation of self-knowledge and the experience of being taken seriously. As the therapy came to a close, the commitment of the survivors in our study to a high standard of integrity in relationships provided a way of maintaining continuity with their pasts, as well as a way of sustaining a hopefulness about their futures.

In the next two chapters, we hope to more concretely illustrate what actually occurs in the therapy by the presentation of selected material from both individual and group sessions. Chapter 5 includes excerpts from transcripts of the individual therapy work. Because of the difficulty in transcribing group material, a more narrative account of portions of the group work will be presented in chapter 6.

*Chapter 5*

# Ceci's First Three Months in Individual Therapy

I n this chapter, we present excerpts from transcriptions of Ceci's individual therapy sessions in the first 3 months of treatment. Our intention is to simply show what occurs in the individual therapy as a way of providing the purest illustration of what we have already presented in more abstract form. In describing what we do at a number of different levels of abstraction, we hope to create a fuller understanding of the treatment process associated with our therapeutic approach. As we mentioned previously, it is not our intention to be prescriptive in any specific way about procedures for therapists to follow.

The material we have chosen represents the same time period for Ceci as discussed in chapter 1. Unless otherwise noted, each excerpt represents continuous material that has been altered only in insignificant ways for the sake of confidentiality and readability. Where ellipses (. . .) appear, they indicate brief pauses; longer pauses are additionally labeled (i.e., *long pause*). The following excerpts are from Sessions 5, 6, 7, and 12, and in each case the excerpt ends with the end of the session. Sessions 6 and 12 are complete sessions.

As mentioned in chapter 1, during Session 4, Ceci had developed an evocative metaphor of her adult autonomy. An imagined living space of her own design served as a counterpoint to intrusive experiences of childhood entrapment. Also of note, about the period between Sessions 7 and 12 as summarized in chapter 1, is Ceci's understanding of the black faceless figure as a personification of her amnesia and prior dread of knowing the forgotten. Ceci gained confidence, during this intervening period, that she could tolerate the therapy process, despite experiences of awakening in terror during the night. She concluded that this faceless presence was challenging but not threatening.

## Session 5

*RB:* I think a core anxiety around being traumatized is that, in effect, it feels unsafe not to be hypervigilant. It is difficult to begin to convince yourself that you may actually be safer, in adult time, to operate out of a calm caution rather than a hypervigilant mind set. It may take a while to convince yourself of that. There may be something about being on high alarm that may resonate with what you had to do to feel safe. One way we could learn more about those implications would be—if you're comfortable today, or we could do it later—is to revisit your internal reflective space again and to see what logic or other ramifications get played out. I think in the long run it's going to be wise not to shrink back from the task of saying, "Hey, wait, I do deserve to feel like I have a secure safety in the world, and although it may not feel that way, it may empower me to be more calmly in control of my life." It could be easy to say, "I'm just going to stay hypervigilant and forget trying to relax my cautions." I think that's the task that you're up against.

*Ceci:* Yeah. Well, I would not be adverse to trying it again. I really feel like I got a lot out of it the last time.

*RB:* OK, well, let's do that while we have some time. I think it may potentially give us a better handle on what you can do to secure that space.

*Ceci:* OK.

*RB:* We'll start at five like we did last time . . . so you can begin to use your breathing . . . slow your pace as you deepen your breath, maximize the release that comes with letting your breath out slowly, four, . . . with each breath an inward turn, your attention more within your reflective mind, the central place, three, . . . using your capacities to visualize as a way to find a focal point within your central focus, now two, . . . a gathering breath at one. . . . OK, why don't you begin with describing the situation?

*Ceci:* *(the pace of her speaking is much slower)* It's the same basically as it was last time. I'm here in this apartment . . . It doesn't feel as bright and cheerful as it did before. The doors are all locked and everything . . . *(long pause)*

*RB:* Try to reflect as to what might help you re-secure your confidence.

*Ceci:* *(long pause)*

*RB:* Describe what comes up.

*Ceci:* I was thinking that in some ways I want a guarantee . . . like, "No one's going to come and get you and kill you." Of course there's always that chance, but the likelihood is that it won't happen. You know I feel like I always operate on that chance. I feel like at least here in this space, I want an absolute guarantee that nothing is going to happen to me. And I don't know, like last week, I felt like I could give myself that, but now I'm kind of wavering like, well, maybe there is the chance that this won't be completely safe either . . . *(long pause)*

*RB:* Follow your associations about that.

*Ceci:* I just started feeling sort of desperate in that sense of . . . It

*Ceci's First Three Months in Individual Therapy*

seems very childish to demand security. I think I'm always sort of doing that, going back and forth between the adult understanding that none of us has complete security and wanting a guarantee that nothing bad will ever happen to us. That's my childish feeling of needing that, wanting that, having to be assured and not getting it. I feel like somehow no one ever assured me that everything is going to be OK. I think about God and my faith, and one reason I have faith or I try to have faith is the idea that this world does make sense in some way, a way that I understand, that it does give me this opportunity to give myself over to God and say, "OK God, I trust you, this will come out better than I think it will." I even have a hard time doing that. It's just a really serious conflict that I have.

*RB:* It seems like you're not sure that you're going to ever easily have say-so over your well-being, that you have to do something very active to demand that you're secure. And, in a way, what I hear is the loss of the assumption of security in how you go about your day.

*Ceci:* Yeah, definitely no, I never assume my safety. It's just not something I'm comfortable doing. I kind of feel like if I did, the moment that I let my guard down a little bit, I'm going to get caught.

*RB:* That's what maybe happened after our last talk. It sounds like for a moment you felt how nice it is to assume your safety, and then all those cautions came up.

*Ceci:* Yeah, that's how I am. I definitely don't feel safe right now. There's part of me, there's this voice that's saying, "This is an illusion. You can fool yourself into this, you can talk yourself into this, but the truth is that you're not safe, and all you've been doing is trying to put a smoke screen up to make yourself feel better."

*RB:* So this is a "helpful" voice promoting high caution and vigilance?

*Ceci:* It doesn't sound helpful! It's much more mocking, much

*Naming the Shadows*

more menacing. It's the voice that says, "I'm going to stop you no matter what."

*RB:* Say more about the sense of threat.

*Ceci:* It's laughing at me and saying, "You know this is ridiculous. You're going through all of this, trying to convince yourself that you're really OK and you're not, you know you're really not." It's like this voice is the voice of the truth. It's the same voice that makes me feel like I'm fat and ugly whenever I feel I'm comfortable with how I look. Or it's the same voice that says I'm mean and nasty whenever I feel OK and that I'm a good person. I feel like without this voice, I pretty much accept myself as I am, but this voice always comes back and says, "Wrong, you're pretty pathetic to even think that you can be OK because you're not, and you're no bigger than I am. I can always come back."

*RB:* I get the sense that this is a running conflict between you within your mind.

Ceci: Yeah, yeah.

*RB:* There's a quality of degrading and humiliation that's reflected . . .

*Ceci:* Yeah, yeah, definitely someone that's laughing at me.

*RB:* You know, it may be really hard at this point in the conflict to understand how this voice has been a help to you, but if indeed you faced degradation and humiliation from the outside that you couldn't control, it may be that you used your creativity to say, "If I learn how to degrade and humiliate myself, at least that will put me in control of when it happens, or how it happens." The conflict may now be inefficient or out of date, but I'm going to ask you to not immediately assume that this isn't potentially a helpful aspect of how you adapted to a difficult situation. Why don't you share your reactions . . .

*Ceci:* I'm not sure how I feel.

*RB:* What's occurring to you?

*Ceci's First Three Months in Individual Therapy*

*Ceci:* I can't really put my finger on it.

*RB:* Does that voice respond to what I said to you or to what you said?

*Ceci:* I think it pretty much only listens to me, and I guess I was wondering if it has ever protected me from danger before . . . *(long pause)*

*RB:* Is that a new question for you?

*Ceci:* Yeah . . . *(long pause)* It's interesting, too, because I did, I don't think I told you. One of the things I'm doing is this creative writing workbook. It has you do these exercises where you write as if you were your internal voice, as your internal critic, the one who has always told you your work is worthless, and to give that critic a voice and to write as if you were that person. And I did that and that voice said, "I'm only trying to do this because I love you. I'm only doing this because I'm trying to protect you." Frankly, I think that's bullshit. I don't think so, I don't believe it, really.

*RB:* Well, without you having a context in which you can understand how it may be adaptive, it's hard not to feel just sort of embattled.

*Ceci:* I feel like that voice is really cowardly, it doesn't want to face things. Its answer to everything is to shut up. I don't believe it's doing it out of love, I think it's doing it out of fear.

*RB:* Well, that will be something to explore. In some ways that's a much more questioning stand, to think that it's out of fear rather than out of malice. It may be helpful to pursue your questions about that. Is there anything we can do, or anything I can help you with in the next couple of minutes to help you find a place to pause and secure what you need to. . . ?

*Ceci:* I don't know, maybe I should give up on this idea of feeling safe. I mean, I feel moderately safe. I guess that's the best I can do right now . . . *(long pause)*

*RB:* OK, try to trust your intuition about that being the best you can do. Try not to force beyond what your intuition tells you is the best you can do, and trust that. Do you have any questions for me before I help you focus up?

*Ceci:* No.

*RB:* It sounds like you're finding a balance that feels moderately relaxed yet holds some room for caution and guardedness, but also for a sense of safety and control. OK, let's start at one and try to move your attention from that balance out into the world, two, . . . allowing your awareness to be more to the office, three, . . . bringing that sense of control and resolve into your adult time and place now, four, . . . five.

*Ceci: (starts coughing)*

*RB:* You OK?

*Ceci:* Well, I don't feel as good as I did on Friday.

*RB:* Maybe it's a more workable balance, not to get swept away with absolute ideas. Try to secure this moderate balance between caution and more discriminating decisions about when you can relax and when you need to keep your guard up, whether that's from person to person or situation to situation. To actually be where you can flexibly raise it or lower it may actually be what's going to work rather than feeling that it's all safe or that there is no security anywhere.

*Ceci:* OK.

## Session 6

*RB:* Catch me up on what has been happening.

*Ceci:* Oh gosh, I'm really sorry I missed last week because I have a lot of stuff going on. I've had a series of dreams. I had three dreams in a row that were really bizarre both in their quality, their length,

and their content. I call them virtual reality dreams, like not knowing I was dreaming until I was awake. They were so vivid, clear, and
realistic. I wrote them all down, and they go on for pages. They
would go on for hours and hours, all these really strange things.

*RB:* This was all in the last week?

*Ceci:* I always dream pretty lucidly and I always remember my
dreams, but these were really serious dreams, real involved dreams
that had real special qualities to them. There wasn't anything—I
have them with me—overtly sexual or violent in them, except one
had episodes of violence, a lot of stuff that I thought were clues, and
in the last dream that I had, I had a dream within a dream. I thought
I had awakened and was saying to my boyfriend, "I just had a dream
about this stuff," and he said to me in the dream, "That's because
you're trying to tell me what it means," meaning the dream that I
had had the night before. And I said, "That makes sense," and he
said, "You're trying to tell me what it means." I really felt like I was
trying to tell myself something. I've been looking back with Martin
[boyfriend], looking for themes and what some of this stuff might
mean. It's hard because I am preoccupied and disconcerted with the
idea of my grandparents' house. It seems to be very central to all of
these dreams. I don't know if you remember me telling you the story
about seeing a ghost in my grandparents' house when I was alone,
and how I'm always sort of afraid to be upstairs alone in their house.
That unsettledness has come back. It has been in all of the dreams,
this house. In the two bedrooms in the upstairs of my grandparents'
house—I think I've said this before—the closets are connected. At
the back of the closet, there's a little passageway that goes to the
back, so you can get between the two rooms without going out in
the hallway. One of my dreams was about being on a team of people
looking for secret passageways in people's houses, and going into
their closets and stuff. It's just so hard because I don't want to con-

vince myself of anything, but this just keeps coming up. Another thing that my boyfriend reminded me of was that about a year ago, I very vividly dreamed about my grandfather molesting me, but I totally denied any relevance. I decided that it was just a dream and that it had no bearing on reality whatsoever, and that there was no way my grandfather could have done that to me. I just completely dismissed it offhand, even though it was a really upsetting dream. Martin brought that up and said, "Do you remember that that happened?" And I said, "I do." I realized that I'm sort of avoiding that. And so, I guess you could say that I'm starting to suspect my grandfather. That's been really difficult because, you know, what if I'm wrong? Finally, Martin just said, "You know, you're not accusing anybody. You have the right to question and that's OK. If your question comes up no, then that's OK, but just give yourself some space to think about this. You're allowed to think whatever you want; you're not doing anything." So I've been allowing myself to think, "What if?" Or is there anything else that's strange about this? Again, you know, I'm just terrified of being wrong. That's really obstructing my thinking about things. I know my grandfather is a really nice man and everybody likes him, but I've always been really scared of him and have had a volatile relationship with him.

*RB:* Which side of the family is he on?

*Ceci:* He's my mom's dad. I just don't know. Again, I have no memories. But this whole thing about their house just keeps coming up. In one of the dreams, Martin was sleeping in one of the upstairs rooms. I was trying to get him to help me. I was going somewhere, and I wanted him to help me. So I was trying to wake him up, and he wouldn't wake up. I needed him to help me. And in that dream, when I went upstairs, my brother was upstairs. He was naked. He was in the bathroom, but the door was open. But when he saw me, he shut the door and told me to go away. So I had this sense of him

*Ceci's First Three Months in Individual Therapy*

protecting me. It was in the sense of he was saying, "Get out of here," but I wouldn't because I knew Martin was sleeping in one of the rooms. I went to try to wake Martin up, and I couldn't. So that was the end of the dream. It was really upsetting. In another dream, another night, I was with a group of people and we were going home. The home that we were going to was my grandparents' house. And then I turned around and went back. I didn't go in. But it just keeps coming up. And the other dream was about secret passageways and looking for secret passageways in people's houses. So this seems to be one of the things that ties in the weird dreams . . .

*(several minutes of dialogue are deleted here)*

*Ceci:* I had dreams on top of dreams on top of dreams. I remember them so clearly. The dialogue was really clear. I have a neighbor who is a good friend of mine who is in a lot of the dreams. I think that that is very significant. Her name is Ellen. She, her husband, and one of her kids have been in my dreams over and over again. I think it's significant because she's someone that I really admire and care about. I also think that she's a terrific parent. She has a three-year-old and a one-year old. She's this really, really, really wonderful mom in the way that she interacts with her children. I love her kids too. In some way I identify with them or want to be like them, or want to be around them. There's something very strange about my relationship with them that seems very comforting. I just like them and like to be with them. Their family seems so healthy and safe. Even though she's not much older than I am, I think of her as older because she's married and has kids in the house and the whole thing. She's like in her thirties. She keeps coming up in my dreams. In the dream where we were looking for tunnels in houses, there was a guy in the dream who knew Ellen. He was black and he introduced himself to me and he said, "I'm Ellen's third." I didn't know what he meant by that. That was very disturbing to me. That was the end of

*Naming the Shadows*

the dream. I've been trying to figure that out. I told Ellen about the dream. She thought it was pretty funny. So I've been trying to figure out what that means. I think that's very meaningful too, whatever that does mean. Then another night I dreamed that I was at Ellen's wedding. Their daughter was there too. At the wedding I was showing her pictures of my family, but I couldn't recognize them. I kept misnaming the members of my family. That was really weird too. I know it just goes on and on, and it's so convoluted. But it just seems ripe with meaning to me, and I can't figure out what it is. I keep reading over what I wrote, thinking about the dreams, trying to relive them, trying to figure out what the meaning of them is. But again, I feel so guilty. I don't want to assign meaning. I mean, of being sexually abused. I could attribute a whole bunch of meaning to these things, but I don't want to do it that way. I don't want to force myself to believe something that it might not mean. On the other hand, I want to try to follow my feelings and explore what I think it means. But I can't let myself do it without punishing myself with guilt. That's why I think that I've started to have nightmares again, like serious ones, like the "bloody shooting" kind of nightmares I used to have all the time. I definitely think my subconscious is very punishing, and when I get too close to figuring things out or doing things that I need to do, I have this very strict, stern punishment clause that comes into effect. I start what I call a backlash syndrome. As soon as I start to feel safe or start to feel like I'm doing something right, part of me comes back and says, "You can't do that," and frightens me or pulls me back. I've been having these dreams, and I've been thinking, "What if this? What if this?" I've started to have panic attacks and nightmares again. I'm trying to keep myself from figuring out anything or really thinking about stuff. So it has been an eventful last couple of days.

RB: You've really been absorbed.

*Ceci: (laughter)* Yes. Well, what do you think?

*RB:* Well, there's almost inevitably a back-and-forth movement as you come to entertain disturbing questions or begin to feel closer to saying, "Hey wait, I think this is pertaining to real events." You'll almost always have the "backlash" reaction. It possibly begins to tell you how doubt has functioned in your psychology as an adaptation. I think we had touched on this in terms of having a critical voice before. It's important to observe uncertainty and doubt as potential information rather than as a problem per se, because in fact every time that you have gotten a bit closer to feeling sure about something, it sounds like your guilt is one way that you buffer against a conclusion. We want to work to see the positive function that guilt is playing, and also help you navigate that in a way that doesn't require that you continue to have to punish yourself.

*Ceci:* Yeah. I told them in group last week that especially since I didn't go home for Christmas, everyone in my family really has been wonderfully nice to me. Everyone keeps calling me. My mom sent me all these clothes, and that's been really hard on me. They've just been wonderfully happy and supportive, and the good family, and that's again fed into my guilt. It made me feel like I really am this terrible person. Here I am taking part in this study and making all this stuff up, and I can't believe what an awful daughter I am. It's just really hard not to have those sorts of reactions like, I am just a big fat horrible person. My brothers, I can count on my hand the number of times I've talked to my brothers in the past few years, and now they've taken to calling me every week just to chat, and that's scarily unlike my brothers. Now they're saying, "How come you never call me?" They're just not people that I call, not people that I chat with, and that's really upsetting me. What are they doing? Are they trying to act like the perfect family because they sense that I am sort of moving away from them? Or am I just wrong about my family, like the things I've said about my family, being distant, emotionally distant from my family? Is that my fault? Am I wrong? It's just kind of strange, so I've had a hard time as far as feeling like a fraud, like I'm making all this up and don't have any real problems. It's hard to remember when I'm on the Prozac that I used to have panic attacks constantly, and that I never had a good night's sleep ever because I was so panicked. And now that I'm not doing that, I'm thinking what's wrong with me, I'm perfectly fine, why am I complaining about anything? How could I possibly be suspecting anybody of doing anything bad to me? It's hard to keep that perspective that I'm here for a reason. So, anyway, that's what I'm doing.

*RB:* Was this the first Christmas that you weren't at home?

*Ceci:* Yeah . . . *(long pause)*

*RB:* I think you're having some trepidation about authenticity. You begin to doubt your perceptions, believing that you're having trouble, for no reason, receiving what on one level feels like kindness being directed your way. Kindness in an uncomplicated family situation usually is pleasurable without anxiety. It sounds like there's still a lot of anxiety if your brother calls . . .

*Ceci:* Yeah, a lot of anxiety. So that's where I'm at. But it's still kind of frustrating. I mean, I feel like things are happening, but they're all so vague. I still can't name anything, and still don't remember anything in the sense of being sure.

*RB:* OK. I think it's good not to jump to conclusions and to think of this period as a time to gather as much information as you can. I think what we probably ought to do today is have an inside reflective talk, and see if we can get some perspective on the punitive and doubting viewpoints that you have. That may help you navigate what sounds like a lot of new information coming at you.

*Ceci:* OK.

*RB:* Any questions?

*Ceci:* No.

*RB:* We'll use the same breathing approach initially, start at five and begin to try to start to pace yourself to a slower, more inward, reflective focus at four, . . . maximize a sense of release as you let your breath out slowly . . . OK, deep breath in, release . . . OK, now I want you to begin to use your visual ability as a way to anchor yourself as you move to your central reflective space, two, . . . allow yourself to be more within now, deep breath, gather yourself, one, . . . being there. OK, try to settle into your reflection and begin to describe what you're paying attention to. Try to follow your associations, and describe them to me.

*Ceci:* It's night now. I'm just sitting with the light on, with a lamp over my head, like a spotlight, but much softer. I feel calm, contemplative. I do feel safe, even though its nighttime . . . *(long pause)* I'm really just sort of settling in and releasing all this stuff, feeling more safely protected, I don't have the frustration any more.

*RB:* As you release the frustration, do you have a perspective on what the frustration has been?

*Ceci:* I don't have a perspective on what it is, but I definitely sense that it's coming from outside of me. You know, what I'm doing when I'm in this "room" is blocking all that out. That's part of the things that I lock out when I lock this door. I get the sense that it's like a spirit, like a gas, like something that's floating that can't get in here. I see it as a vicious and a dangerous thing, something that envelops me in daily life. Here, I definitely have it on the outside. And so I'm sort of, I'm not really scared of it, but it's just such a burden that it feels good to lock it out. But I don't really have a sense of where it comes from.

*RB:* You picture it as a gas?

*Ceci:* It's like it's floating. It almost has a face, but it doesn't really have a human face, more like an animal, more like something you put

*Naming the Shadows*

on over yourself. It reminds me of Indians, you know, when they put skins of animals or animal heads over them to disguise themselves. That's what it seems like, it's outside my room floating there, and if I let it in it could come and just land its head on my head and cover me up, and just seep right into me. But it can't do that right now.

*RB:* It feels good to be in charge of defining your own boundary of privacy.

*Ceci:* Yeah, it's almost like I don't need it, the gas. It almost feels like an obligation in my regular life. And here I can give myself permission to say, "OK, in this one tiny spot, you don't have to wear this." Yeah, that feels very good. It sort of seems like some sort of obligation. Part of being a person, part of being me, is that I've taken on this obligation to wear this thing, and I don't like it. I feel like I've made some sort of deal to wear it, but I can't remember what it was. So here in this space, I feel like its some sort of free space where I can take it off without having to renege on the obligation. I'll put it back on when I leave here.

*RB:* I get the sense that you feel like that although you forget the origins, you feel like you've made some sort of deal that leaves you feeling obligated to wear a different identity or disguise.

*Ceci:* Yeah, or just like the guilt itself. I don't feel like the guilt and punishment and frustration are part of me, part of who I am, but for some reason I've traded something for the obligation to wear this. And so I have to, it's like honoring that obligation . . . *(long pause)*

*RB:* As burdensome as it is, it's impressive to know that you're someone who stays true to her obligations. That may be a positive way of looking at it.

*Ceci:* But it's also fearful. I feel like if I did renege, then something really terrible would happen. It's not just my sense of honor. I feel like if I threw off this cloak, I would die or something really terrible would happen. That's the deal that I've made.

*Ceci's First Three Months in Individual Therapy*

*RB:* That's the part that doesn't feel like you've really chosen this deal.

*Ceci:* It's sort of like the lesser of two evils. It seems like either something catastrophically bad will happen, or I'll choose to wear this guilt. So I choose to wear the guilt. You know, it doesn't seem like much of a choice. And yet I do still have this sense that I know that, on the one hand, I can break out of it. There is still part of me that sees that this is something that I could overcome. It's a threat that's not going to become real. That's the struggle. There's a part of me that knows that I'm stronger than this, but part of me is really afraid to test that possibility.

*RB:* The sense that something catastrophic will happen may actually be out of time rather than current-day reality. You may be remembering the logic of an out-of-date anticipation.

*Ceci:* Yeah. I get into spots, like here in this place, and there are other places and other times where I feel like I can take it off for a minute. That's part of the rules. It's like I'm just skirting the rules, just following the letter of the law. So I can take it off and be OK. But I can't really defy it. I can't really say, "No I'm not going to wear this anymore." Suppose something catastrophic happened, because I do believe that. I do believe that something will happen. And you're right, it might just be that I'll remember something, but it's not going to be fun, it's not going to be pretty. If I say "No more," then something is going to slam back in my face. So I'm sort of caught between the real need to know what that is, and the real fear of what the price is going to be. You know, what is going to be the catastrophic thing that's going to happen to me? It's really hard. I really fluctuate on whether I'm ready to do that or not . . . *(long pause)*

*RB:* I get the sense that you're moving closer to a place where it's not so much that you can't remember what happened, but you're not sure whether it would be safe to remember.

*Naming the Shadows*

*Ceci:* Yeah. I think about my grandfather and I have this feeling of falling off a cliff. It's just so overwhelmingly atrocious that I can't fathom it. I can't think about it in any constructive way. And I don't know whether it is the terror that it *might* be true or the terror that it *is* true. So I can't think about it directly. That's what it's like. It's like a cliff. If I let myself remember something and it's true, and I'm past wondering whether or not it's true, then it is like falling off a cliff. It is like, that's it. Once that starts, then I have to deal with everything that that brings up. I'm going to have to deal with whether I'm going to tell my family. I'm going to have to deal with how they're going to react. I have to deal with what that means about all my relationships. It would automatically change all my relationships with my family members. It's kind of like looking into that chasm, but I don't know if I'm ready to jump off yet. And I can't take it back. If I remember something, then it's real. Then I can't say, "No I didn't really remember that." As long as I don't remember anything, I can say, "Well, I have my feelings, but . . ."

*RB:* It often feels that it would irrevocably change your relationships. I would argue that it probably doesn't change them so much as clarifies them. Although on the surface, you might maintain the hope or a sense that this is a positive relationship. To know may bring clarity to this attachment confusion that's mixed with anxiety and obligation.

*Ceci:* Yeah, I've been thinking of that in terms of my nuclear family, and now also in terms of my grandparents. I perceive that there's a rather large gap between the relationships that we *pretend* we have with each other and the relationships that we *really* have with each other. We have this perfect family, yet I don't feel any reality there. I don't feel any real emotional connection to my family, none of them really. My younger brother is getting married. He just announced his engagement, and so my family is gearing up for the wedding. I realized that I have a great anxiety about large family events in our family because we have a whole family myth of how our family does things, of what our family is like, and how we put on parties and celebrations. I find a huge falsity to it. I feel like that's not reality, that's not really the way we are. We're not really that close. We don't really know each other at all. So I have these huge discrepancies in my mind between what I'm supposed to go along with and what is real. I feel that in relationship with just about every member of my family. There's the acceptable surface relationship, and then there's what goes on underneath, mostly nothing. Underneath it all it's empty. Underneath it all there's nothing there. That's exactly how I feel. Underneath all the pretense, there are no relationships. We don't deal with each other at all. So it's really possible anything could have occurred underneath the surface, because the surface isn't real and I know it isn't real.

*RB:* OK. I think that enlarges an understanding of what you started out with, a sense of what is being covered by imposed, but not real, identity appearance. The guilt or shame may be an internal experience of participating in the pretend, of what helps you put it on, when underneath you have many determined strivings to be honestly present. Why don't we find a place to pause. I get the sense that underneath there's a yearning to steadfastly participate in non-shrouded, real attachments. There's a sense of danger about that, but also healthy excitement. Do you have any questions about this before we focus up?

*Ceci:* No.

*RB:* OK, why don't we start at one, . . . move your attention from your workplace, bringing that at-peace-with-yourself balance more present, two, . . . use your breathing in reverse to structure your attention to the outside, three, . . . more into the morning, more present-day, four, . . . and five, . . . focus.

*Naming the Shadows*

*Ceci:* (sighs) Well, that seemed productive.

*RB:* Give me some feedback.

*Ceci:* I was kind of surprised that I was so vocal, that that kind of stuff came up. I was sort of shocking myself as I was saying that stuff. That was really productive. It started to make me think stuff that I hadn't consciously realized before about my family. The making the deal of wearing the guilt is something that I've never even considered before. I mean, that really just came out of left field. So yeah, it's kind of a lot to process, but I do think that was very helpful.

*RB:* The thing that strikes me about you is when you talk from that safe-enough-to-be-honest voice, there's a very clear thinking, strong-willed kind of mindedness about you.

*Ceci:* It's part of the being safe, of the being able to explore, to be able to say, "OK, I don't have to explain everything, I don't have to apologize for everything." It's given that what I'm saying might not be the truth, fine. I think I'm able to put that outside and say, "OK, here I am and I'm just going to say what I think without the disclaimers." That's the one place I feel like I can do that. It's kind of interesting to see what comes up when I don't have all the other noise in my head, without all the 'shoulds' that I always have with me. That was really neat. That really made me feel a lot better. I feel really good now.

*RB:* Well, we'll keep working at it.

*Ceci:* All right.

*RB:* See you next week.

*Ceci:* Thanks.

## Session 7

*Ceci:* I guess in a way it sort of brought up the fact that my image of my family as perfect is just as wrong as my image of my family as monstrous. It's somewhere in the middle of that. The letter was a reminder that I'm not completely off base that there's some strange stuff going on in my family. So in some ways that was helpful, but in some ways it was a painful reminder. So that's what I've been dealing with for the past couple of days.

*RB:* It sounds like the strongest feeling was anger about hypocrisy.

*Ceci:* Yeah. I think he [father] had every right to be upset that all of his kids forgot their mom's birthday. I think that's clearly our fault, and he certainly didn't know I was going through a hard time. So I certainly think he has every right to be upset by that, but the way he did it I thought was very cowardly and hypocritical and it really, really, really made me angry. It just set stuff off again. I've had dreams, but not any more strange dreams or strange feelings, not anything monumental like I thought was happening last week.

*RB:* Why don't you give me some follow up. You were saying last time that while we were in the reflective dialogue that you felt a certainty about the dreams and the questions.

*Ceci:* The whole thing that I said about feeling the guilt come off me, and being able to see it like it was a coat or a skin left outside of my room was illuminating. I think the part where I said it was part of a deal that I made to wear this coat, it's something I've never said before. I really believed that was the truth. I realized that was something that just came out of me. It wasn't something that I made up, and I really believed it. And even though afterwards I have doubted the validity of that, I was so certain when I said it that it startled me, it surprised me that I said it. It's like it came out of nowhere. I was telling Martin about it later and he said, "It doesn't surprise me. It's the first time you said it, but it's not something that surprises me, given what I know about you and your family." So that made me feel better. Also, what you said about me sounding very clear and direct when I was speaking was right. I felt very clear and direct. It wasn't

*Naming the Shadows*

very difficult to say the things I said. It seemed like it was all there in a way that in normal consciousness I don't feel. I'm constantly questioning myself, constantly thinking, "I'm evil, evil, evil. I'm making this stuff up," you know? But then when I was in the reflective view, it was like, "This is the way it is whether I want to believe it or not." You know, there wasn't any of that confusion. Again, it was like a taking off of the coat, putting it aside for a second, and being able to be in touch with what I felt without trying to censor it or judge it. I knew what I felt. I was very sure of what I felt. The whole thing about making the deal that I had to wear that coat or something horrible would happen to me, I knew that was the truth for a minute. I knew that I was telling the truth, and there was no question in my mind that I was telling the truth. And so that was difficult, but it was also sort of affirming. I felt better after that, like, "I'm not making this up." That was really powerful. I talked a lot about it in group last week. When I told it in group, I said, "Even now I feel like I'm making all this stuff up," but at the moment I said it, I believed it was true. And they all said, "None of us thinks you're making this up. Every one of us believes you." That sort of brings me into a really strange realm. It's just weird psychologically feeling like, "Am I crazy?" I guess that's part of another explanation. I pretty much know I didn't make this up. I didn't consciously make up anything, but I'm not convinced it's the truth. So I feel like in some ways, maybe I'm just a lunatic. Somewhere in between, I have this strange perception of reality. Do I believe something that never happened, or did it happen? I guess it's possible that what I remember happened, or something about what I remember happened. But I think I am progressing. I think of it as a strange realm of reality when I think about this kind of stuff. I have this book at home about repressed memories. I've looked at it before, and I looked it over again

*Ceci's First Three Months in Individual Therapy*

this week. It addresses things like believing that you're telling the truth. And it says that if you're more worried about being a liar, then you're probably not lying. If you're really concerned that what you're saying isn't the truth, then probably it is. That helps in some senses and not in others. It doesn't really make me that much more convinced that I'm telling the truth, so . . .

*RB:* It seems that what you're really describing is two different arguable mindsets that you carry, and you see how dissonant the two are in comparison. It's either "something crazy happened or I am crazy," and they don't fit together.

*Ceci:* I alternately believe that either one is real, and I can feel myself sort of scrunch in and out of those realities. It's got to be one or the other. Both of them are rather uncomfortable to believe. It's not fun to think either one of those things is true, so I can't really decide which one is really true . . . I hope I'm not crazy. I keep telling myself that in the rest of my life, I seem like a pretty sane person. I mean, I manage to function in all other realms of my life, in reality. I think I deal with people pretty well. I deal with my job pretty well. No one's ever accused me of being crazy. I feel like I have a grasp on reality in other ways, so that helps me . . .

*(several minutes of dialogue is deleted here)*

*RB:* Do you have a sense of where you want to head today?

*Ceci: (pause)* One of the dreams that I had had was about being in that mental institution, visiting my friend Stan's ex-wife who had been sexually abused, and having feelings that I had been in that mental institution before. One of the things that I had written in my journal was that the walls of the institution were rough, like they were under construction, like they weren't plastered or anything. I then realized when I was reading that over that they were the walls of the attic in my grandparents' house. That's what they were like, unfinished, and the insulation . . . This was very upsetting to me and very startling. I seem to be having a lot of references to my grandparents' house. I can't get past that. I don't know where to go with that.

*RB:* Do you want to spend some time talking within a reflective focus and see where that leads? It sounds like there are some threads and some questions.

*Ceci:* OK.

*RB:* Start at five, . . . begin to pay attention to your breathing, locating a deeper breath. Maximize a sense of release with each breath. Finding a slower pace, four, . . . with each breath now, allow yourself to move more within your gathered mind, your reflective mind . . . deepening your absorption there now, there, . . . you may want to begin to anchor your movement with your central space. Use your visual abilities to allow yourself to be more within what you see there, two, . . . even more there now, collect yourself, deep breath, one, . . . OK, why don't you start to describe what you're paying attention to.

*Ceci:* It's the same room. I am just being in a part of it. It's night again. It's strange. I can definitely see the coat of guilt that I've left outside. I feel safe and OK.

*RB:* Pause for a moment and try to begin to pay attention to what in your intuition and wisdom feels like an important direction, maybe not so much try as allow yourself. Follow your associations and begin to describe what occurs.

*Ceci:* Well, I think that I feel compelled to look back at my grandparents' house, why I have a lot of fear associated with it, and why it keeps showing up in my dreams. I'm just kind of picturing it. My grandparents live in a very small town. It's a brick house, kind of a normal house. Like I said, the upstairs was just one big attic, but it has been converted so that it has two bedrooms. If you went straight up the stairs, there are four doors. There are two doors that lead directly into the attic and two doors that lead to the bedrooms. The bedrooms are connected by a closet. There's a bathroom upstairs. The kids slept upstairs. My mom had two brothers and two sisters. There is eighteen years between my mom, who is the oldest, and her youngest brother, so they didn't all live there at the same time. That's also where we kids slept when we came to visit and still do. I've always been afraid to be up there myself. I remember there's a door at the bottom of the stairs. That's what makes me think it was an attic. You can shut the whole upstairs off from the downstairs. I remember, I used to wake up really early. We couldn't come downstairs until seven o'clock. I just remember sitting at the top of those stairs, waiting to be allowed to come downstairs because I just hated to be up there by myself. It was really spooky up there. I guess when I stayed there, my two aunts were still quite a bit older than me, so I was the only one who slept in that room. When I was very young my youngest aunt would sleep up there too, but she went to college. So mostly I was alone up there. It was just a really spooky place. I hated it. Another thing that's bugging me is that I know so much about being in that attic, about being in that closet, but I don't ever really remember going in there. I don't remember why I would go in there. I do remember my youngest uncle used to go through there and scare us, playing. That's not a particularly frightening memory. It's kind of a funny memory, you could hear him coming. I can pretty well picture what it looks like, with the closet and the little door. The attic space was really cold because it wasn't heated. And the door on the other side opening into the closet . . . It's just really frightening to me, but I don't remember why I went through there.

*RB:* One thing you may want to try is to allow yourself to focus within the scared, cold feeling that you're drawing to mind and just let your mind associate. It doesn't necessarily have to make sense, but just see what that feeling brings with it, the associations.

*Naming the Shadows*

*Ceci:* It's funny, I can remember, it's so vivid to me, the temperature of it. The chilliness of it. It even smells strange, kind of damp and musty, a very particular scent, not like any other place I've ever been. And the walls, the walls are like insulation and wood. The insulation has a foil wrap on it. It's shiny. It's cold to touch. That seems strange. I definitely can feel what the walls felt like. I can picture my hand on that insulation, that metal sort of foilish feeling, but again I don't know why.

*RB:* Why don't you try to linger with that sense of your hand on the foil and see what comes to mind.

*Ceci:* I can picture—I can feel my hand on it, and it's really dark in there, pitch black in there. I have the sense that I'm in there by myself. I have absolutely no reason to be in there by myself. I'm young. I can see my hand and it's definitely a child's hand. I can tell what direction I'm in. I can tell that I'm coming from my aunt's room into my uncle's room. I know which way I'm facing.

*RB:* What else do you notice?

*Ceci:* Just feeling kind of cut off, almost like that space is independent of any other space, like it's not part of my grandparent's house. It could almost be on another planet. It's just its own space and time. It's just there. I'm afraid. It's cold, it's dark, it's creepy. I don't know why I'm there.

*RB:* Tell me more about your sense of being young.

*Ceci:* All I can see is my hand. It's a small hand. A five- or four-year-old hand, not like a "baby" baby, but like a small child's. I know it's my hand. But that's all, I don't have any other sense of my body except for that hand. I'm just kind of touching that wall. I don't know, but I do feel like I'm heading towards my uncle's room.

*RB:* Why don't you see if you can allow a sense of time to move forward and describe what happens next.

*Ceci's First Three Months in Individual Therapy*

*Ceci:* I want to say that I go through there and go into my uncle's room, but I don't know if that's true.

*RB:* Try and stay within the moment. Don't think your way ahead of yourself. Just try to allow it to evolve.

*Ceci:* It's almost like I want to move forward, but I can't. I'm stuck there. It feels like it would be a relief if I could get to my uncle's room and get out into their closet, but I can't. I can't leave there.

*RB:* Take a deep breath and settle yourself while we explore this question. What might prevent you from moving?

*Ceci:* I can't. I'm not held there, I don't think. I feel like I'm suspended there. It may just be fear. It may just be that I'm afraid to. I don't have the sense that I'm bound or anything. I do definitely have the sense that I want out, but I can't get out. It's almost like somebody told me that I couldn't leave there, and I'm afraid to leave because I've been forbidden to leave. Yeah, that's what it feels like. I do have the sense that I'm alone in the dark. It's cold, and I can't leave. I'm scared. It's almost like somebody put me there and said, "Stay there or else," and I can't go.

*RB:* Suspended in terror with a directive to stay . . .

*Ceci:* Yeah.

*RB:* What comes to mind about that?

*Ceci:* Actually, I started to get this feeling just now of things fitting together. I'm terribly claustrophobic. I'm scared of being stuck in places. I'm scared of elevators. I'm scared of airplanes. I'm not scared of tunnels, but I'm scared of being in tunnels where there's traffic, very specific fears, phobias of being trapped. And it's making a lot of sense to me all of a sudden. I know I told you when I first met with you about my enduring fear of being a prisoner of war. My fears became so urgent the night the Gulf War started that I cut off all my hair. It was like I was on automatic.

*Naming the Shadows*

RB: A larger picture begins to feel connected . . .

*Ceci:* The other thing that's strange is that it definitely feels self-imposed. I don't feel like I'm locked in the attic. I feel like I've been forbidden to leave, and the fear comes from considering disobeying whatever that is. I can get out if I want to, but I'm afraid.

RB: What comes to mind about being afraid to disobey?

*Ceci:* Well honestly, my grandfather comes to mind, just the terror of him. The fear of being in trouble. The fear of him. I don't know. At first I was thinking, maybe I'm in the attic to hide from him. I can't decide if I'm there because I don't want to come out. It feels more like I'm there because somebody told me I had to stay there. Yeah, because I definitely don't want to be here, I definitely want to leave. So it's not like I'm hiding. So it's as if somebody said, "You have to stay here," and I'm just terrified that I'm going to be in big trouble if I come out.

RB: Describe more what this image of your grandfather that scares you looks like.

*Ceci:* I just saw his face. My grandfather is a very big man. I've always found him frightening. He is very tall, very broad, huge hands. He's a nice man. He's jovial, but he can be very stern. I've always felt very frightened of him in that aspect. I've always felt frightened of large men. You kind of get the impression that he could just break your mouth with his hand. I don't have much feeling towards him. When you said, "Think about what you're afraid of," I flashed to my grandfather. That doesn't necessarily make any sense to me.

RB: For a moment, try to relax your thinking and just follow what comes up.

*Ceci:* It's strange because I feel like in my regular life, I have no memories of being a child. No actual memories in which I feel like I'm there as a child. And here I do. I can feel what it's like to be really small and afraid, unprotected and trapped. Even memories I do have of my childhood are as an adult looking back on it, like it's a movie. But I can definitely experience myself here.

*RB:* It's different to have experienced it from a younger perspective.

*Ceci:* Yeah.

*RB:* Why don't we take a couple of minutes to find a place to pause. Are there any other ideas or questions that you might have before we focus out?

*Ceci:* No, I'm OK.

*RB:* OK, what I want you to do now is use your breathing to create a movement from the time and place of the attic when you were four or five. Allow yourself to move to your central space, the apartment, as a reminder of what being in a room in the present day as an adult can be like. As you allow yourself more presence here, describe what you notice.

*Ceci:* I'm just back at my apartment in the city. I'm at my desk. I'm definitely having the urge to write now.

*RB:* OK, be sure to give yourself time today to do some writing.

*Ceci:* Yeah. I'm doing OK. I feel fine.

*RB:* OK, we'll start at one, . . . begin to use your breathing in reverse now to move from the balance you feel inside, your attention out into the world, two, . . . the here and now, three, . . . allow yourself to be fully present, the morning, four, . . . and even more here, five . . .

*Ceci: (sighs)*

*RB:* . . . a really different experience where you feel connected to your youth.

*Ceci:* It's very vivid, very strange. Wow.

*RB:* Some ideas, impressions or questions . . .

*Ceci:* I'm just sort of freaked out. I kind of feel unreal. I have this feeling that I know I'm not making that up. I know I'm just trying to remember, to reflect on what's happening. It seems so strange and unreal.

*RB:* What feels unreal about it?

*Ceci:* Again, it's like a liar. I feel like that when I say those things. In the reflection, I know I'm just describing what I feel and what I see. I mean something really resonates with me of a truth. Suddenly my view of all of my fears about being trapped someplace and not being able to get out, just clicked into a broader possibility. But already, as soon as I'm back in the real world I start saying, "Are you just trying to justify your fear?" Already this voice is saying, "Well this is really convenient, you've come up with this nice little story." And so again, it's the same dichotomy. I'm really scared that I might be remembering something important, and I'm really scared that I might be making up something really absurd. Immediately, that critical voice is there saying, "You're making this up."

*RB:* I think that the more you have these incompatibilities, the more that you'll see the potential meaning and function of your viewpoints. Of course, one possible function of thinking yourself a liar is that it helps distract you from experiences that have an intensity and a link to a sense of being young, real, and vulnerable. There's a sense that on the one hand, that's very much what you're yearning to be connected with, and on the other, to be able to say that you're a liar can solve a deeper vulnerability. There's something about younger, vulnerable feelings that can be difficult to stay with day to day.

*Ceci:* It was very vivid, I know exactly what the temperature was. I could see my hand touching the wall, and I know exactly what it felt like. I saw it, I felt it, I smelled it. It was so realistic, not like something I would make up, not like something I would imagine, but something that has a memory to it. I could feel that wall. I could see it, it was shiny. I knew that was real. Why could I see that vision of my hand like that?

*RB:* Well, we'll keep working on those questions. It does seem like it's a provocative counterbalance to your usual viewpoint.

*Ceci:* OK, well off I go.

*RB:* Same time next week?

*Ceci:* Yeah.

## Session 12

*RB:* So how are you doing?

*Ceci:* Good. I've had kind of a good week, just regular, nothing major is happening. I talked in group last week about being here. SR suggested that I might talk with you about my feelings of someone trying to kill me . . . I thought that might be a pretty good idea. I don't know if I would get anywhere, but I am feeling comfortable enough to at least explore that possibility.

*RB:* OK, so compared to a week ago, you haven't had that same kind of intensity of intrusion?

*Ceci:* No, I haven't been waking up. I've only had one more episode of the gagging in the middle of the night. So I'm back to just fine. In some ways I'm also worried that I'm blocking out that stuff. It was getting so hard. I've gone back to just not dealing with it. So I'm not having trouble at all, or it may be, like you said, that I'm taking a breather from it. But I feel like I'm not working, like it's been too easy lately. In fact, I've been feeling really good. I don't know, I guess that shouldn't be bad, but . . .

*RB:* Yeah, don't let that be a worry.

*Ceci: (laughter)* I'm happy that I'm feeling good, but I still feel like I should be exploring stuff all the time, but I think I must have taken a vacation from that.

*RB:* There's value in being able to take a vacation.

*Ceci:* Yeah.

*RB:* Well, do you want to try to not take a vacation?

*Ceci:* Sure.

*RB:* You indicated that you might want to try to explore the whole experience of the gagging.

*Ceci: (pause)* Especially the feeling when I had that episode last week, the certainty that someone was about to kill me. I realized that was a prominent fear before I was taking Prozac, and before I was in the study. Almost around the clock I had this feeling like someone was about to kill me. I'd like to know where that comes from. OK?

*RB:* OK, why don't we start out with getting yourself situated in your central space and honest voice, and then we'll decide how to approach the material. Let's start at five, . . . begin to slow your pace, calming breath, allow a sense of release with each breath, four, . . . allow yourself more freedom to be, to be within your reflective, central mind, three, . . . use your visual ability now to locate yourself more inside, gathering breath, two, . . . being there now, one . . . Start out by describing what you're paying attention to.

*Ceci: (pause)* Just sort of settling myself in. I feel good. The sun is shining outside and the room is very bright. I'm looking around the apartment. I'm looking at it from a new angle.

*RB:* Tell me about the new angle.

*Ceci:* Well, I'm over in the corner. Usually, I start off on the couch. It's like a loft apartment. It's really just one big room. This time I'm over in the corner, in the kitchen corner where there are more windows and just looking at it from that angle. It's sort of like a triangular-shaped room. It's just fine, comfortable, but I'm definitely feeling more active, looking around, walking around, whereas before I was always sitting on the couch. Also, the door is right across from the couch. I have always felt like I was very focused on the door and what was going on there. Now I feel like I'd rather not be.

*RB:* You're secure that the door will remain secure even if you don't look at it. . . ?

*Ceci:* Yeah. I'm just really enjoying this space. It's really beautiful.

*RB:* It seems like you've had a lot of architectural freedom to design a triangle.

*Ceci:* Yeah, it's really weird, the room is extremely detailed. It's not someplace that I've ever seen, but I feel like I know everything about it. I just today noticed the triangle.

*RB:* Try and think of your needs right now. Assess for yourself where you need to be, whether you need to head towards the corner or if there's something else that comes first.

*Ceci:* It's hard because I'm feeling really anxious. It feels like a vacation in a way, like I suddenly have all this energy. I'm just not sure what to do next. I've had this enormous burst of creativity. Over the weekend for Martin's Valentine's Day, I painted him a picture. There's this poem that he really loves. I did a watercolor with the poem and framed it. It was actually really beautiful, and I was shocked. I've been very noncreative, very empty, and all of a sudden I was filled with this creative energy. When things are coming to me, I feel like all my energy is going towards being OK. But now, things are getting flung at me, like at night. I'm feeling really energized to focus on things but I'm not sure where, like I don't feel naturally led in any direction.

*RB:* Let's try to trust your intuition as to where to head. SR's suggestion might be an answer, but I don't want to override your answer. You've had some well-guided wisdom about you to this point. Let's honor that. Be true to that.

*Ceci:* To be honest, I don't think I can get very far right now as far as thinking about what I'm afraid of because I'm not in that kind of mode. What I've discovered so far is that in order to be able to think about what I'm afraid of, I have to feel afraid, and I'm not feeling that right now. I was thinking last night about trying to organize some of what has been going on, like the dreams, and that thing with my throat, and the different scenes that I have, and the fears at night. Since I am in a creative mode, maybe I can see them as pieces of a puzzle and see if they fit into a larger picture. Maybe I can do that here. It seems like at first I started having dreams, and the dreams were very specific. I was having these dreams about my grandparents' attic, and those spooky feelings about that room be-hind the closet in my grandparents' house. Then I remembered hav-ing had that dream about my grandfather's sexual abuse, and also a very specific dream about being in a mental institution and looking for somebody. Then I realized that I'd been there before, that the physical mental institution was actually the walls of the attic. That seemed very hard to deal with, but very plain to me as far as mean-ings go. But then my dreams started getting into these other things, like the whole thing with the black man and this feeling of a missing child, a child that died and that somehow I was facing a grown-up shadow of this child. That seems just as real to me as far as some-thing that's deep and meaningful, but yet much more mysterious as far as what it really means. Then I stopped dreaming altogether and started to have these actual physical sensations, the shaking and the gagging, the feeling of the knife at my throat, and waking up in the middle of the night terrified. To me those are even more abstract. The gagging is real but it's not even like a dream, it's not even a symptom like the fear that someone is trying to attack me. So there's even less of an idea of what this might be in reality. Did someone re-ally put a knife to me or did someone try to kill me or is that the way I've interpreted it? It seems even further from the plausible. I think that's important to me right now, trying to look at those things,

*Ceci's First Three Months in Individual Therapy*

question those things, to see if there's any way that those things could go together, or to see if they fit as part of a set or part of a pattern. Aside from the fact that they're scary, I don't really see anything.

*RB:* You have the intuitive question that these may be pieces of a puzzle. Why don't you see if you can envision it within that form, synthesizing it if possible.

*Ceci:* Well, I already see them visually in terms of closer and farther away. The initial dreams about the attic seem to be placed on a time line much earlier, the black man dreams in the middle, and the choking sensation at the end nearest to where I am now. I have that sense of a time spectrum. In some sense they could be related to the same thing, saying things to me in different ways.

*RB:* What occurs to you?

*Ceci:* In some ways I feel like the initial dreams about the attic and that stuff perhaps represent something close to what did happen to me, or at least represent a danger or a perceived danger that I was in as a child. The black man dreams were sending some sort of reassurance to me that I lived through that, that I'm OK, that I did manage to not die. Yet the choking dreams and the knife-to-the-throat dreams seem to represent to me that there's still some major threat to speaking. And that still has something to do with the idea of time, and one thing following after the other. It seems to be saying, "Something happened to you, you're strong enough to deal with it because you're still alive, but you'd better not talk about it because then you die."

*RB:* Three angles. . . ?

*Ceci:* It's funny because I was just starting to think how I've been thinking about this turning out to be a curve. I was just thinking about how whenever I am drawing or doodling, that I'm obsessed with drawing circles, perfect circles. I can almost draw a perfect circle freehand. I've always wondered why I am so into that idea. That's what it almost feels like, that it's almost started to meld itself. And maybe there's another part to it too. Maybe there's another aspect to that that hasn't been revealed to me yet. It's like this circular logic that keeps me from figuring it out. Part of it that's weird is that the room is triangular. I guess in some ways it's more like a circle than a triangle. The door is at the base of the room, then each of the two corners are on either side of the door. One is like a study area, one is a kitchen area, and straight in front of the door is a loft. There's another room up above, so the loft takes up a major part of the other side of the room. The bed is sort of up against the loft wall. It's really interesting that the bed is up there. You have to take these stairs up there. There's even a door above the bed for escape purposes. It's very clear that it can be locked from the inside so nobody can get in, but I can quickly take it down and get through it onto the roof and escape. So if anyone came into my apartment when I was sleeping, I'd be out of there in a second without any trouble or before they could get me. And when I'm in bed, I can see everything in the apartment. The only enclosed space is the bathroom. It's underneath the loft. So there's no hiding, no scary, secret things. Everything is out there, and that's the way I feel secure. I realize, too, that when I was really scared, like when I was in my house by myself, I sleep in the living room. I want to be in the main part of the house, which doesn't make a whole lot of sense because if anyone ever came in, I'd be a goner. It seems more likely that if I was in my bedroom, if somebody came in the house, I'd have more of an opportunity to phone somebody or try to get out a different way or something. But I need to be where I can see everything, where I can open my eyes and see the doors.

*RB:* There's a sense of entrapment or hoped-for escape that seems most associated with that.

*Ceci's First Three Months in Individual Therapy*

*Ceci:* Yeah, it's like I'm being on guard . . . *(long pause)*

*RB:* So in imagining your room, it gives you some information over what the important anxieties are that you are in the process of mastering.

*Ceci:* It's funny, I've never really thought about it before. I've always thought of it as cool—kind of a neat place.

*RB:* Beside all the anxiety . . . *(laughter)*

*Ceci: (laughter)* I guess that part of the reason why it's fun is that inside I don't feel that anxiety, that's fun.

*RB:* Maybe that is what fun is, right? *(more laughter)*

*Ceci: (laughter)* Not feeling scared or anything. And it's open, too, because it's a loft. The whole thing is like two stories tall, so it very much has the feel of a warehouse, with a lot of windows, so there's plenty of light. But they're warehouse windows with little squares of glass so nobody can break into them *(laughter)*, and it's hard to see out even though there's lots of light coming in. So it's very much where I feel free. I was just thinking of not feeling trapped. This is the complete antithesis of that feeling of darkness, of being closed in, fear of not being able to leave. Here it is open and light. I have several very well-marked ways to leave. The two corners, there's an emphasis to where the two rooms are . . .

*RB:* Go on with your associations.

*Ceci:* I was thinking that the attic, could it have been shaped that way, just in terms of the architecture of the house? It would be because, the two bedrooms were at right angles to each other. So, the space where the bedrooms would meet, the space behind them would be shaped like a triangle because there was a bathroom in between them. It's weird. Maybe it's not and maybe I'm just trying to make myself, make myself . . .

*RB:* It may actually be very telling that in this—although the room itself provides you a sense of safety and freedom—it actually has embedded in it the very danger that you're trying to master in terms of its architectural form or ambiance, anxieties that you're trying to override. What's occurring?

*Ceci:* I'm listening to that noise outside, just feeling anxious.

*RB:* Out in the hall?

*Ceci:* Yeah.

*RB:* What reactions do you have to it?

*Ceci:* A doomed feeling . . .

*RB:* Do you have any associations to the sound?

*Ceci:* No, I just startle easily when I hear a loud sound. It just terrifies me. Ever since I was young. I hate fire alarms. I hate loud noises.

*RB:* Do you think you became more vigilant as you became aware that your imagined room has some connection to this potential traumatic space?

*Ceci:* I don't know. It's hard to tell. I wonder, if there wasn't a sound, would it bother me as much? I don't know . . . Yeah, in some ways, definitely. I'm starting to feel a little creepy, that weird feeling.

*RB:* What does it feel like, creepy?

*Ceci:* Well, every time I have these feelings, I'm still at that stage where it's like "Something is going on here, something different that is very wrong." Certain things resonate with me, like it happened to me. This seems to be one of those things.

*RB:* I have the sense that it maybe caught both of us a bit off guard. You were talking about piecing together three pieces of information and, in effect, we stumbled upon a fourth source of information.

*Ceci:* What's the fourth?

*RB:* The parallel between your sunlit room, a metaphor that you created to evoke a sense of autonomy and security, and the attic.

*Ceci:* The circle. Yeah, that makes sense to me if you put that piece into its place. It's almost like I've taken it back to when it happened to me. I've reframed it into something that I'm not afraid of, and that goes right back to my grandparents' house in the attic and feeling like something's weird. Yeah, that does complete the circle. Something happened, I lived through it, I can't talk about it so I revamp it, and then I go right back to "Something happened." I can't stop that. And each one is just solidly locked into place.

*RB:* What's often compelling, is when you stumble upon understandings where it's hard to think that you could have constructed them. This is one of those moments where the way the mind works is a bit more complex than you and I anticipate.

*Ceci:* It's true. I know I'm not constructing this. I know I'm figuring this out as I go. It's scary how much fits.

*RB:* And it's also reassuring. Obviously I have a more comfortable vantage point, but it's reassuring that your creative capacities are guiding the way, seemingly staying a step ahead.

*Ceci: (pause)* I was thinking how my creativity offers me a sense of pride, and that in some ways, discovering these things through my creativity allows me a sense of strength. Some sort of position of holding it out to myself in terms that I can incorporate slowly, and just this sense of power that I get to interpret it. I get to assign meaning to it however I want to. That feels good. It feels less chaotic. I get to take that dark triangular space that scares me and turn it into a light triangular space that makes me feel safe. It reminded me, too, of the dream that I had where I was both the child and the adult. I was showing my dad what I had written and he said it was crap. I realized what that was like, not just in the sense of wanting my father's approval and not getting it, but also the idea of squelching my creativity because it does allow me to see things that I can't easily articulate. I've always written poetry. I started writing poetry when I was four.

*RB:* One lesson in terms of our work together is that SR or I might have an idea about where to head, but let's always keep that in the context of paying attention to what we know now. We know that you have a creative map that's quite operational, and that's moving you through this your way.

*Ceci:* Yeah, I was just thinking that if I had spent this time trying to think of what I was afraid of, I would have been frustrated.

*RB:* And the paradox is, that you actually stumbled upon your information that begins to answer that for you.

*Ceci:* Yeah.

*RB:* Why don't we take a moment to pause. Do you have any ideas or questions?

*Ceci:* No.

*RB:* OK. Use your breathing as a way to bring your attention out from where your best balance is, one, . . . hold the reassurance that you have a capable guidance system, two, . . . use your breathing to bring your alertness out into the morning, three, four, . . . alert now. Five.

*Ceci:* That was great. I'm feeling really energetic now. I feel really excited. In some ways it's scary, because the information that still comes is serious.

*RB:* You're on top of it, aren't you?

*Ceci:* Yeah, that's really kind of neat. That's good. I won't feel guilty for feeling great, until next week anyway.

## Chapter 6

# Case Narratives from the Group Work

In this chapter, we present descriptions of segments from Sessions 24 (6th month), 31 (8th month), and 46 (11th month) of the group therapy, based on videotapes of the sessions and written with the intention of simply recounting what happened with as little interpretive overlay as possible. The nature of the group interactions are, unfortunately, difficult to convey in transcribed form, particularly since the dialogue is not always orderly, and since the atmosphere is only partially captured in the dialogue. For example, it is not uncommon for more than one person to be speaking at the same time, or for there to be important group emotional reactions that are not expressed in words. We have thus chosen to present, for the most part, a narrative account of the therapy process. We have, however, included verbatim material when we thought it would enhance the presentation.

There was a basic structure to the 2-hour therapy sessions, although there was also a great deal of flexibility about the particulars of this structure in response to individual and group needs in any given week. The basic structure included a "go-around," whereby each member had an opportunity to say how she was doing and to report to the group about important aspects of the intervening week. While it was clear to everyone that the therapy was focused on recovery from the long-term impact of childhood trauma, the topics of conversation were not restricted in any way. The basic structure also included the opportunity for individual members to work more intensively on individual concerns, with the possibility for greater therapist and group feedback. In both these situations, group discussions of matters of common concern were often generated. The amount of time spent in any particular week in these various "activities" was not systematically planned, but evolved during the group process.

Within this basic structure, it was the therapists' responsibility to establish, over the long term, an equitable distribution of "therapy time" among the individual group members and to encourage a group response that was sensitive to the needs of individuals. A norm was established both to respect the value for each individual to speak freely without interruption, as well as to stay absorbed in each other's work in a way that would facilitate feedback and discussion. In any particular week, time was not necessarily shared equally among the group members, even in the go-around.

The first segment, taken from Session 24, focuses on Ceci and describes her presentation to the group of what she discovered on a trip to her grandfather's home during the prior week. This description of Ceci's work in group complements the previous description of Ceci's work in individual therapy and illustrates the continuity of the therapy across the two settings. There is a period of approximately 3 months between the last individual session described in chapter 5, and Group Session 24 described here.

The next portion is from Session 31 and covers the period of the entire session, which was essentially one protracted go-around. Included in the description of this session are verbatim letters written by Caroline, Alice, and Ceci to their respective parents, which provided the centerpiece for group discussion. Although this session is not *un-*

representative, it was not always the case that there was as much of a common thread in the go-around as in this particular session.

Finally, the description from Session 46 is of a segment that includes a group discussion of the broader family contexts in which the members of our group grew up. This illustrates the kind of back-and-forth between members that was characteristic of discussions, which were in contrast to individual presentations both in the go-around and in the more intensive work.

For all descriptions, it helps to have the following picture in mind: SR, her cotherapist, and the members of the study are seated in a circle. Everyone is serious, but not somber, and there is a clear sense of intimacy among the group members. Everyone appears to be intensely engaged in hard work.

## Session 24

At the start of this group, everyone knew that Ceci had just returned from a visit to her grandparents' home, and people were anxious to hear about her trip. Ceci started the group off by saying that she had had "quite the trip," and that she had returned with pictures of the attic and a long story to tell. She was asked by SR if she could wait until after the go-around, and then take an hour to speak. It was also suggested that she could give a brief overview at that point. She said she was happy to wait, and that she would just say at that point that her youngest aunt had disclosed to her that she, her aunt, had been abused by Ceci's grandfather and had retained memories of the abuse. Another aunt was in therapy because she had suspicions that she was abused, although she was unable to remember anything specific. This aunt's grown children, Ceci's cousins, had amnesia for their childhood.

*Naming the Shadows*

About an hour later, after the other group members had had the opportunity to check in, Ceci began to tell a powerful story, without interruption, for approximately the next 30 minutes. The story was essentially about what she had come to understand as a result of visiting the feared attic at her grandparents' house and talking with family members. It was told in a way that made her mastery of the impact of what she had learned evident and striking. It was told in a way that was also very interpersonally engaging, because the tone assumed a strong connection with the group. It was a story that Ceci urgently wanted everyone to hear, all at once, without stopping to answer questions, so she could get it all out without losing her concentration. The members of the group seemed to listen intently, out of concern for Ceci and with an ear toward what they could take away about their own therapeutic work.

The following is Ceci's story in our words. We have not entirely respected the sequence in which Ceci presented information, and we have not held true to the level of detail of the original version, partly out of concern for Ceci's privacy. We do not believe, however, that we have distorted the meaning of her story in any significant way.

Ceci started her story by repeating the information that she had disclosed at the start of the group about the evidence put forward by her aunts for her grandfather's abusiveness. She then prefaced her day-to-day account of her trip by saying that this was not the only thing she had found out. Upon her arrival at her grandparents' house with her boyfriend, Martin, she had been struck by the accuracy of her detailed memory of the attic space, right down to the writing on the insulation with the foil wrap. Martin had taken pictures of the attic space, and Ceci showed and described these pictures to the group. She expressed her excitement about the pictures and about how "freaked out" she had been upon first seeing the attic.

Before describing how the disclosure by her youngest aunt had come about the next day, she filled in the group with some background about the names and ages of her mother's siblings. Ceci's youngest aunt, who we will call Toni, was quite a bit younger than Ceci's mother, and only about 10 years older than Ceci. Toni had always remembered that she had been sexually molested by her father, who was Ceci's grandfather. She had kept this knowledge a secret until 5 years prior, when she had approached her older sister Terri, and she had always worried about whether other members of her family had been sexually abused by her father as well. She told Ceci how she had worked to establish closer ties with certain female nieces in the hope that they would open up to her if something had happened to them. She was not surprised to learn of Ceci's suspicions of abuse by her (Ceci's) grandfather, and deeply regretted that she had not somehow been more protective. The initial exchange of information between Toni and Ceci on the second evening of Ceci's visit, as described by Ceci, seemed to be accomplished with a great deal of ease and warmth.

Ceci returned to her grandparents' house that same evening, having planned to sleep there for a second night. She woke in the middle of the night, terrified that she would be killed by her grandfather. She and Martin packed their things at 3 a.m., and waited up for an appropriate time to leave in the morning. Ceci described the irony of her early morning conversation with her grandmother, just prior to leaving the house. Ceci's grandmother told her how someone in the neighborhood had been forced to call the police in the middle of the night because they heard a neighbor beating his wife. Her grandmother then expressed to Ceci how she could not understand how someone could stay with a man like that. Ceci told the group that she didn't know at that moment whether to laugh or "kill" her grandmother.

Ceci and Martin considered heading back home then and there,

*Naming the Shadows*

but Ceci decided she would rather stay around to gather more information. She was looking forward to meeting with her other aunts, particularly Terri, in whom Toni had confided. She was also thinking about confronting her grandfather at that point, although she came to realize that that was unrealistic given her commitment to Toni and the fact that Toni was not ready for a confrontation. Over the next several days, as she spent time with her cousins and aunts, Ceci came to know quite a bit about her family that she said she had not known before.

She described to the group what she was told about her grandfather's life. Her angry tone in the telling of this part of her story came, according to her, from her recognition of the hypocrisy in her grandfather's assertion of his moral purity, and from her realization that the keeping of family secrets, even within the family, was commonplace. For example, some members of the family were well aware of her grandfather's long history of extramarital affairs and alcoholism, and his own abusive upbringing. Ceci also described to the group stories she was told by her mother's sisters about her father. According to Ceci, her father, like her mother's father, often judged others with an attitude of moral superiority, even though the lack of integrity in his own behavior would be apparent under the same kind of scrutiny. The implication of Ceci's words and tone was clear. She had not before been helped to see the ways in which her family was very troubled. In fact, the trouble had been covered up for the sake of creating a sense of security in false appearances.

Ceci's confusion surrounding the secrecy in her family was poignantly illustrated by her description of a "bizarre" disclosure to her by Toni. Toni told her that her father (Ceci's grandfather) had told her when she was a child that she (Toni) had had a sibling who was born dead, and that she should never mention it to anyone, especially her mother (Ceci's grandmother). Ceci had had an intuitive sense for some time that there had been a death of a child in her family, and Toni's story had the ring of familiarity to her. Ceci had the idea that she was told the same story by her grandfather, but intuited now that he had told the story to both her and Toni as a test of his power to keep them quiet. What she described as the *most* bizarre aspect of this disclosure was what she learned about her mother's reaction to Toni's recent inquiry. Ceci had asked her mother some time ago if there had been a death of a child in their family. More recently, Toni had independently asked Ceci's mother the same question. Ceci's mother denied any knowledge of such a thing, but surprisingly didn't seem to make anything of the fact that she had been asked the same question now by two members of her family. The question was about a tragic public event, and warranted, in Ceci's mind, a very different reaction from her mother, regardless of whether a death in the family had actually occurred.

While Ceci's account of what she had learned on her trip was told with expressions of the kind of strength that comes from a confidence in perspective, her account was not without references to the vulnerability she experienced during her week-long visit. For example, she described how she spent a sleepless night after hearing about her grandfather's life and experienced a need to "get out of her body." She had felt she could not be around reminders of her grandfather any longer. On her drive back home with her boyfriend, she decided to tell her parents, who lived in a different city from her grandparents' home, that she needed some time and distance from them in order to sort out the overwhelming nature and amount of information she had gathered. Her parents' reaction, which in her mind was lacking in both respect and compassion for her needs, likely contributed to her continuing experience of vulnerability upon returning home.

Ceci described to the group how, upon returning from her trip,

*Naming the Shadows*

she had awakened in the middle of the night to the terrifying sense of being in her grandparents' attic. It had taken her some time to realize that she was safe at home in her own bed. She described how she had been having urges to drink heavily and cut herself, and how her grandfather's presence had invaded her "workplace" in the first session with RB after her return home. Her grandfather's presence was intensely felt there, literally as well as figuratively, by the sense of his hands touching her shoulders. It took some time for her to get control of intrusive imagery during this session with RB, and she understood that RB was generally concerned about her sense of safety. She described being frightened by RB's reactions to her during the session, reactions that expressed how seriously he took what she was describing to him. Ceci was scared by the thought that he was scared, and it was her description of the session with RB that began the group discussion of her moving story. The remaining 30 minutes of the group was a series of interchanges between Ceci and the group members and SR.

Most of the discussion centered on issues of self-knowledge and hopefulness about relationships. While Ceci's current vulnerability was acknowledged in a compassionate way, the group response was more focused on the obvious strength and courage reflected in what Ceci had described. The group members clearly understood the feelings of power and pride associated with a commitment to honestly facing a painful reality. They understood, too, the relief in the realization by Ceci that she wasn't crazy and that the best way for her to understand herself was to persevere in piecing together a life narrative. It was clear that this wasn't a task to be taken lightly, and SR supported RB's cautions about staying safe and relying on her current trustworthy supports, both in the therapeutic environment and outside of it, to do so. The group members understood, in Ceci's case as well as their own, both the fear and joy in being taken seriously in the context of ongoing and future alliances. RB's reaction to Ceci's story, as contrasted with her family's dismissiveness, provided, according to Ceci, an important reflection of her own experience. She realized, after some thought, that he wasn't scared.

In the course of discussion in the last half hour of the group, Ceci expressed her confidence in her ability to draw on her current relationships in order to care for herself, as well as her ability to set limits in those relationships that she felt were destructive. She also expressed her sense of responsibility to consider the needs of helpful others who themselves were affected by what she was going through, as well as her sense of responsibility toward children in her family who remained at risk for being abused. Before the session was over, the discussion turned to the protection and care of children more generally, ranging from the endearing qualities of children to appropriate child-rearing practices. All the members of the group felt secure in their opinion that a child knows the difference between an interaction when an adult does something that is in the child's best interest, and an interaction when an adult simply asserts his or her authority to some other end.

## Session 31

Before describing this session (characterized by an extended go-around), we will briefly describe the events of the week before, which provided an important context for this session. Session 30 of the group therapy took place, in effect, in the emergency room of Duke University Medical Center. Although the group session wasn't actually held in the emergency room, the interactions of group members and group therapists that followed from hearing about Caroline's car accident were, in our view, therapeutic. SR took advantage of an opportunity, due to an unfortunate turn of events, to communicate indirectly about the nature of trustworthy relationships. While SR's actions were in no way ingenuine, and while the conventional structures of therapeutic work were absent, SR maintained a therapeutic role in the sense of self-consciously creating possibilities for highlighting important therapeutic messages in a different setting.

As we waited in the usual group room for several members to arrive, word came that Caroline had been in a car accident only moments before, and even though she seemed to be doing fine, she had been taken to the emergency room for observation. SR, her cotherapist, and the group members made the decision to go to the hospital to see how Caroline was doing. Once there, arrangements were made for everyone to visit with Caroline, and the incident was characterized by the group members as exemplifying the kind of "family" relatedness they all cherished. The presence of the group therapists basically provided a stamp of solidarity to the group as a whole, as SR and her cotherapist were just quietly present. The hour or so at the hospital gave the group members some food for thought about their own families, as is evidenced by the topics of discussion in Session 31.

Caroline started the session off by reading a letter she had written to her parents but did not intend to send because it was too "ugly." She prefaced the reading by saying that she wrote the letter after her realization the week before that her investment in the group seemed more worthwhile than her current investment in her relationship with her parents. She described the letter as very meaningful to her. It has been changed in insignificant ways to protect Caroline's privacy, and reads essentially like this:

### Caroline's Letter

*I'm not happy to write this letter, but I feel that you have left me with little choice. I do not wish to communicate with you right now. I'm very angry*

Case Narratives from the Group Work

with you, and I feel that you know that, and yet you persist with your chirpy little, "Are you OK?" messages. And the truth is, you really don't care how I am. You only care that I be the way you want me to be. You don't care about me being OK, you only want me to make you feel OK, and to tell you the truth, I'm sick and tired of it. You don't help me feel OK, why should I help you? I'm tired of the long-suffering parent role you are trying to pull off, and I'm sick of being the family crazy so that you can go justify writing me off. What am I angry about, you ask, as if you don't know. I will humor you. I was traumatized as a child under your care by you. I was physically, verbally, and sexually abused by you. And yes, I'm angry about it. I don't know what you thought you were doing as parents. Maybe you thought you'd never be held accountable. Because we were your children, we would have to accept whatever garbage you dished out. Or maybe you just thought we deserved it. But I'm an adult now, and I'm holding you accountable. I do not have to accept your garbage, and I do deserve to be taken seriously. What am I angry about? Maybe that even though I've told you all this, you continue to act as though nothing's happened. I've tried many times to talk this all over with you when I first became aware of the abuse, but it has been clear to me that you do not want to hear what I am saying. You only want to deny it and cover it over with stupid little presents and fake "I love yous." Right now I don't even trust you not to talk about it. Take, for example, the gifts and the cards. Are they bribes really? I have received from you lately a Snoopy sweat shirt with a small label in the back that reads "troublemaker." I tried to overlook that one. Then came the cards—Mom's flimsy attempt at "peaceable kingdom." Thank God it's something different you're offering, Mom. And Dad's "Having a great time. The state for lovers. Wish you were here." Not exactly the best of wording coming from a father whose daughter has told him he sexually molested her. Let's see, there was the "big bucks" cordless phone. More money than you've spent on a birthday gift for me in a long time, huh? The card reads, "Call us." And then last, but not least,

*Naming the Shadows*

*comes the video* Homeward Bound. *It was a cheap shot, but you couldn't resist pulling those heart strings one more time, could you? Oh, and how can I forget the pictures [of her nieces]. It's just like you to recruit them to do your dirty work. I'm not buying the whining grandparents' pleas for my daughter's love either. Why am I angry? I have asked you to leave me alone for a while, but you have not done it. You have hounded me and needled me. You have insulted my intelligence and played games with my emotions. I do not think this is what a family should be. It is not what I want for myself or for my daughter. You are not a family for me. You are not there. Do you want to know how I am? I'll tell you. I'm doing great. Better than I ever have. I made the dean's list at school—straight A average. I have been offered several positions. I bought a car. Alison [daughter] is learning to swim and to read. And I have friends who are very dear to me who care about me, listen to me, and like me just the way I am. My life is not perfect, but I like it. I like it a lot, and I don't need your judgments of how it's going. Contrary to how I am sure you are presenting it to others, I am not trying to hurt you. You are responsible for your behavior. I am merely dealing with the truth, and when you are ready to deal with the truth also, I would be most interested in listening to you. Until then, I'm not playing sweet games with you. I will not be talking with you or sending you pictures or even writing you any more letters. If this is painful for you, I am sorry. It has been extremely painful for me as well. I have spent untold amounts of energy, money, and time trying to understand why I have felt and acted the way I have for the last 25 years. There are not words to express the grief and loss I feel over my brother. There is no way to tell you how I have missed the companionship of my siblings who are still alive and yet who will have nothing to do with me. I feel betrayed, I feel cheated, and yes, I feel you owe me something. You owe me the chance to know you as better people than you have been and are. You owe me the truth. And until you are ready for that, I will have to move on. (end)*

After reading the letter, Caroline talked, in a self-reflective way, about how writing the letter had initially made her feel like a bad kid. She then described how she had begun to understand that she was hard on herself, in the sense of driving herself too hard, taking blame for things that weren't her fault, and not looking out for herself more. She talked, for example, about being intimidated by the oversexualized behavior of her boss at work, and how it was difficult for her to stand up to him. Caroline then shared with the group some reflections about her high school years. Sometimes she read from a journal she kept that related to her work in therapy. She was looking back, trying to make sense of what she recalled of her behavior and feelings. She remembered how fragmented her experience of life was, and also the comfort associated with the gentle wisdom of a special teacher, and with the church. For the most part, the other members of the group were quiet during Caroline's "turn," only occasionally interrupting with a question or a supportive comment. Caroline brought her turn to an end on her own after about 25 minutes by reading one of the recent letters she had received from her mother.

Alice took her turn next, and as she was preparing to read a letter she had sent her parents, there was some joking among the group members about their engaging in "show and tell." There was a clear excitement about sharing the kinds of experiences that signaled progress in their work, and everyone was eager to hear what Alice had to say. Alice, in an atypical fashion, had not sent her parents Mother's or Father's Day cards, or a card for their anniversary. Her mother had left a message on her answering machine, on Father's Day, saying essentially how worried she and her father were that they hadn't heard from her, how much they loved her, and that they were thinking of making a trip to see if she were doing OK. Alice had transcribed the message that her mother had left, and read it in full to the group. The threat of being intruded upon by them at a

*Naming the Shadows*

time when she wanted distance prompted her letter, which she also read, and which she had faxed to her parents during the previous week. The letter (changed in insignificant ways) follows:

### Alice's Letter

*Mom and Dad. Happy day-after-father's-day. Everything's fine. I'm OK, Tom's OK [boyfriend], Spanky's OK [pet] and even clean. We gave him a bath yesterday. My job's OK, Tom's job's OK. My fingers [job-related injuries] are status quo. I've heard nothing else about the settlement [worker's compensation]. I've just been busy and nontalkative. Don't worry. Alice. (end)*

Within hours of receiving the fax, Alice's mother called. She said receiving the fax had helped, but wanted to know if Alice realized that she had not written "Dear" Mom and Dad, or signed it "Love" Alice. Alice said she realized those things. Her mother wanted to know what she had done wrong. Alice said that she didn't do anything recently, that it was something from the past, a long time ago. Her mother asked her if she was "getting back memories." Alice said that she thought it was something her dad may have done. Her mother asked if it had anything to do with *her*. Alice said she wasn't sure yet. Her mother began crying hysterically, and her father took the phone. He wanted to know what she had said to her mother, and scolded her for making her mother cry. He then started making small talk. Her mother then got back on the phone and said they had planned to make a trip to see her, but guessed they shouldn't surprise her. She said they shouldn't. Her mother said she would only come if it were OK with Alice, and that they would plan the trip. The conversation ended there.

Alice described to the group how she had, at first, felt powerful for having been able to stay true to herself in conversation with her mother. By the end of the day, however, Alice was feeling guilty, worried about destroying her family, and generally awful about the impact that her mother's reaction would likely have on the rest of the family. A card arrived from her mother not long after their phone conversation. While on the surface the card was loving and supportive (e.g., "To our daughter, with love forever," and "Call us when you are ready"), in the context of the phone conversation it made Alice angry. She felt that what she had said on the phone about what might have happened to her as a child was being ignored. After recounting some dreams she had had following the phone conversation, she described how she had written in her journal that she could not excuse her parents' behavior, even if they had had a hard life. She noted that this was a change of heart for her. She had written that she was angry at them for not responding to obvious signs of her distress when she was a child. Alice's turn ended with a group discussion of how necessary it is to look out for yourself, and stand up for yourself, so that you are taken account of and not taken advantage of in the service of someone else's needs. SR's contribution to the conversation was to congratulate Alice on how she seemed to be feeling less powerless.

Alice, like Caroline, had taken an extended amount of time in the go-around, and as sometimes happened, the expectation was set that the go-around would fill the group time. It was Ceci's turn next, moving around the circle clockwise, and she, too, had brought to the group a letter she had written and sent to her parents. She began by stating that she had had an eventful week, one that rivaled the week when she had visited her grandparents' home. She then read the following letter (which has been changed slightly to protect confidentiality). It was addressed to her mother.

## Ceci's Letter

*I have decided that enough time has elapsed and enough distance created that I can write this letter to you. I have to admit that I am very sad that*

*Naming the Shadows*

*while you have made your displeasure with my silence very clear, I have felt very little sympathy or concern with what might be wrong, except those very vague suggestions that I might be seriously troubled. Actually, I'm doing fine. In a lot of ways, I've never been better. I'm trying to come to grips with my past, and contrary to what you believe, I know I am strong and independent enough to deal with it and move on from it without placing the blame on other people for my own problems. But just because I take responsibility for my own life does not mean that I will refrain from being angry or distancing myself from those who consistently hurt me and put me down. For the past three years I have been struggling with the fact that I was sexually abused as a child. I know you will not believe this, and I don't care. But just to answer your first reactions, I am not a liar, I am not mistaken, and no one talked me into this. I am not a victim of a psychological fad. I am also not accusing you or my father of being my abuser. This is a fact, and one that I take very seriously, and if you cannot also do so, I advise you to stop reading right now and continue to have nothing to do with me. I can do without your hysteria, your condemnations, and your accusations. The reasons I asked for some space before telling you this are several. First of all, if you think about it, you will surely agree that our family has a history of trivializing and avoiding anything serious that is facing us. I have been trivialized and avoided enough, and I needed to assure myself that I am not looking for your sympathy, your confirmation, or your permission. I know what has happened in my life, I am taking steps to heal it, and I don't need your support. You have a right to know, so I am telling you. In addition, although I do not blame you for my abuse, there is a very upsetting tendency within our family to pretend we are perfect and everything is fine. Everything is not fine, and I refuse to call and chat or otherwise pretend everything is normal while I am struggling and you are pretending not to notice. That was what was driving me crazy. One thing that pushed me out of contact was the fact that I was having a hard time, you knew I was having a hard time, and yet you were content to not say anything, and to never ask me what was wrong or show any concern. I can't take that. Finally, I have chosen to write this letter to you and only to you. You may show it to whomever you wish, but I purposely did not address it to my father. He told me he does not care if I ever talk to him again, and I do not care to talk to him. He has not dealt with me for years, so I am over the rejection. But I refuse to pretend that we have any relationship at all. I would appreciate it if you would stop signing your letters "Mom and Dad," because Dad had nothing to do with them. If he ever wishes to forge a relationship with me, he can write his own letter. I also had to laugh when you referred to the abuse he heaped on Toni for no reason, and tried to claim he never treated me that way. Don't insult my intelligence. I know this letter is hurting you, and it is not my intention to do that. But if you really want to know me, and know what is bothering me, this is it. It's not pretty and it's not easy. I have a great deal of anger and pain also, and I am done thinking that it is wrong of me to feel this way. You said there was nothing I couldn't tell you, so now I am telling you. If you want to talk about it, you are welcome to write me. If you do not want to talk about it, you are welcome to not write me. I won't be expecting anything, and I will not write again. Please do not try to call me, and do not try to have your friends and relatives call me, because I will not respond. I do hope that some day we can re-establish a relationship, but it will take a lot of work. Having an adult relationship with your child has nothing to do with proximity, and everything to do with the willingness to listen in ways you never have and may not want to.* (end)

After reading the letter, Ceci described what she had just found out from her Aunt Toni in the way of additional evidence for her grandfather's sexual molestation of children. She also described the steps that Toni had taken to protect the remaining young children in the family from Ceci's grandfather, and how additional family members were coming to take the situation seriously. This made her feel as though she had a family and that there were people in her family whom she could count on. She did not include her father in this mix, and she went on to read a lengthy letter from him that she had just received in response to her letter to her mother. Her father's letter was angry and shaming, accusing her of being self-absorbed and blaming her for not appreciating the heroic parenting efforts of her mother as well as the caring and sacrifice from him on her behalf. He did say he was willing to talk. Ceci noted several times that he did not say anything about the sexual abuse.

There was considerable discussion by the group about Ceci's letters that largely focused on a clarification of what the letters meant to her. For example, Ceci described how she understood better now what had made her afraid of her father in the past, and how she now saw her father's behavior as being driven by his own guilt. Ceci also expressed her disappointment that her mother had not responded to her letter. She was asked by SR to say what she understood about her mother's lack of response, particularly in the context of her father's mean-spirited response. Ceci said that her mother was probably just letting her father "take care of it," and while her mother in all likelihood knew that her father was angry, she probably hadn't actually read his letter, adding that her mother, upset as she must be, was just too weak psychologically to respond.

The contrast between the power Ceci now possessed and her description of her mother was evident throughout the discussion. She described a dream in the course of the conversation that captured so well who she now was in relationship to her traumatic childhood experiences. She and Martin were taking a plane trip, and they were taking a baby with them for whom they often babysat. When they reached security at the airport, they put the baby down on the machine, and the baby got trapped and began to cry. The man operating the machine was so upset that he just ran off. Everyone else was

*Case Narratives from the Group Work*

standing around saying, "What are we going to do? Is the baby going to die?" Ceci ripped the metal and glass machine apart with her bare hands and rescued the baby, who was fine. She had realized that she somehow had to do what was necessary to protect the baby from any further harm.

Jesse's turn took the remainder of the group time, although group was extended to give Jo a chance to at least do a quick check-in. Jesse was feeling very depressed, and spent most of her time describing how she was not the person she wanted to be and did not have the kind of life she wanted to have. Her lack of felt connection to anyone seemed particularly salient to SR from the outset in Jesse's tone and in her words. For example, as she talked about her reaction to the fright of Caroline's accident, she said, thinking of her own mortality, "I could die, and nobody would know."

Jesse had alluded at various points, as she talked, to such things as "a clean slate" and "a new beginning." After Jesse had talked for some time, SR decided to ask her about this language, and the conversation wound up touching on a number of important thematic issues for Jesse. The dialogue that follows is continuous and leads to the end of Jesse's turn. The material has been altered in insignificant ways for the sake of confidentiality and readability. As before, ellipses (. . .) indicate brief pauses.

*SR:* Why do you need a clean slate? What's the matter with the slate you started with?

*Jesse:* Because I always feel like I'm having to fight uphill battles, that there are obstacles I've put in my own way that now I have to fight harder to get out of the way, instead of just moving along at a steady pace, you know? That's what I see other people in life who— I mean, their big problem is, yes, getting a job, just like everybody else, passing the exam, just like everybody else. But, you know, their arguments with their parents are over curfew, clothes, boys, *not* unmentionables. And husbands and wives argue about miscommunication, at the worst, and the trivial things, although they're important and break up things, like money. Paul [husband] and I never argued about *anything. Anything.* We argued about stuff in our head. I mean I'm sick of these . . . *(sigh)*

*SR:* But you say a clean slate as if you screwed up or something. Clean slate means you get another chance.

*Jesse:* Yeah. I did—do feel like I screwed up, yeah. And it may not have been my fault that I screwed up, but I still screwed up. If somebody makes you lame and you trip, you fall behind. It's *you* that tripped, even if you weren't the one who shot yourself in the foot.

*Ceci:* What if someone kicks you, though, and holds you there?

*Jesse: (pause)* Yeah . . . but that still feels to me like I'm shirking responsibility for my life. That's just how it feels.

*SR:* What if somebody shoots you in the foot, and you keep walking?

*Jesse:* I'd like to.

*SR:* I mean, why not characterize it like that, as opposed to somebody shoots you in the foot, and if you fall down, it's your fault? Why wouldn't it be, somebody shoots you in the foot, and you keep going?

*Jesse: (long pause)* I guess I wouldn't be able to blame myself, but I'd still be disappointed in the progress. I mean, I just feel like I'm backtracking, you know? I'm tired of—

*SR: (interrupting)* You'd be angry, right?

*Jesse:* Yeah. But you're hindered by your own anger. You're hindered by everything. You'd be hindered by the pain. I just want life to be—

*SR: (interrupting)* Don't you see a lot of people angry in a way that doesn't hinder them? I mean, don't you see Ceci angry in a way that doesn't hinder her, that's just more that powerful image of saving that baby, or, you know, I think she would've done the same thing at the emergency room.

*Ceci: (to SR)* Surely you would've. *(group laughter)*

SR: I guess part of it is that anger can be powerful as well as defeating. It depends on whether you feel like it has a hold of you or you have a hold of it.

*Jesse:* It's baggage. It's stuff you've got to drag with you. So on every new trip—

SR: *(interrupting)* Yeah, but that's like the clean-slate business.

*Ceci:* You seem to be blaming yourself for things that people did to you.

SR: Also, you want some continuity in your life. You don't want to have this idea of yourself that you have to start from now and get rid of all the—

*Jesse: (interrupting)* I don't want it to matter anymore that I had a miserable childhood.

SR: It's part of who you are, right?

*Jesse:* But I don't want it to hinder my life, you know?

SR: Well, that's fine. But that doesn't mean you have to kill it.

*Ceci:* The way I translate it with my dad is, you know, look how far I've come. I'm a human being. I'm a functional human being, despite the fact that that man's my father. *(group laughter)*

*Caroline:* Also, I think there's something about science that teaches a lot of false dichotomies. Everything's either-or. Everything's put in this category or that category. You don't have to either put it behind you or let it rule you. You can find something in between, in the middle, that you're comfortable with.

*Jesse:* Yeah. Nothing is comfortable. It's always towing a fine line. The other thing I forgot to mention was I called my mother. My brother's twenty-seventh birthday is the thirtieth, and I don't even have his phone number. And part of this is, why the hell should I call him if he can't even bother to give me his phone number? But part of me says, you know, I want to. Fine. But all of you have been besieged with parental attention. *(group laughter)* My mother hasn't called . . . I haven't had any contact with my mother since I yelled at her in the dorm's common room at my brother's graduation, which was a full month ago. That is the longest time my mother has gone without calling me. And, I don't know, I feel like it's a very empowering kind of feeling when you can say, "I don't need my parents anymore." I think I went through that a little too early. It wasn't my decision not to talk to them. It was Paul saying, "You need to get angry at them and you can't talk to them anymore." And after a while, my father apologized, my mother seemed to accept it, and I wanted to just rebuild something. And the stupid thing is that I got suckered in. I believed all that. And then when Paul and I split, I felt like my mother was the only one there for me. Why would she be close to me now when I've never been able to be close to her when I was in the same house?! But, when you feel like you need somebody, and I'm saying I'm not going to be suckered in anymore, *not going to be suckered in anymore*. But I called her to get my brother's phone number, and she just goes, "La la la la la," and talks about this, that, and the other, like the pear tree she planted has been bearing lots of fruit. *(group laughter)* She's into her landscaping and stuff. And I'm saying, "Well, you can't eat all the pears because you've got to pluck some of them so the other ones get better." And she says how it's such a little tree, and it's so heavy with fruit, and she feels sorry for the tree. And I'm like, "OK, this is just charming." It was so innocuous, you know? And I almost felt charmed by the innocuousness of it. And I say, "No, Jesse, don't get suckered in just because you feel a sense of connection. This is your *mother*, even if you're never close to her, even if she's a ding-bat, even if you can't believe what you're discussing on the phone, which is this poor little pear tree that has too many fruits." *(group laughter)* But it's a sense of, "Gee, it's kind of nice to be able to talk about nothing with somebody." Except that with her, you can't talk about *something*. And I'm saying, "I can't get suckered in by this again. I can't. I can't. I can't." And the person I really want to talk to [husband] just totally misunderstands me and tells me what's in my head. So, it was just like a poignant feeling of I can really be suckered into thinking I have some kind of a relationship with my mother even though we can't discuss anything. Just a feeling of, well you know, good feelings, good will, forgiveness. We just can't talk about anything of substance. And then I see her in person and I can't stand it.

Before group ended, Jo told them about her week, which had also been very intense emotionally. She had fallen down some steps and hurt her back so badly that it was hard for her to care for herself. She described how difficult it was to get help from her husband and how she had wished the group could have been there. She had felt as if she was with family in the emergency room the week before. She had found out in the past week that her own family had lied to her about her uncle coming to a family reunion, as we mentioned earlier. Jo described a flashback she had had during the week, that she had also had previously, about her uncle's sexual abuse of her. She said she felt more ready to talk about the abuse and work on it at this point.

## Session 46

As was noted in chapter 4, we came to understand more completely, in the second half of treatment, the full extent of maltreatment in the childhood environments of our study members. Session 46, which was in the 11th month of treatment, was the first time our

*Naming the Shadows*

study members discussed as a group the kind of physical discipline that was normative in their homes.

Around 45 minutes into this session, Alice started her turn and soon began recounting stories about aspects of her mother's personality that had been extremely difficult for her to deal with while growing up in her parents' care. One of the things that was a focus of her stories was her mother's violent outbursts, which led to an hour-long discussion among the group members of the physical abuse they had endured in their childhood families.

Alice's description of her mother's fits of rage was contextualized in her broader characterization of her mother as troubled and inept at providing the comfort and guidance expected of parents. Although her father was physically abusive as well, her mother's behavior was experienced by her as more out of control. Alice's descriptions of her parents' behavior were received by the group members with the kind of understanding that comes from shared experience. Her tone did not initially convey the seriousness of what she was describing, but the course of conversation over the next hour clearly revealed the seriousness of the violence in the homes of the group members. Even though the language varied from "spankings" to "beatings," by the end of the discussion there was agreement that their parents' behavior was outside the range of what would normatively be considered acceptable, even among those who believed in physical punishment.

In sharing their reactions to being hit by one or both of their parents, the members of the group discussed both actual and hypothetical situations. They talked about how it felt emotionally as a child to be hit by a parent, how they remembered having comforted themselves, and how they behaved toward their parents in response to being hit. The meaning attached to different reactions was an important focus of the conversation, and in considering this, they talked about how they would feel and react if they were to be hit by one of their parents in the present day. Their discussion of their reactions to each others' stories also provided some insight into their own feelings and aided their ability to understand why they reacted the way they did. Caroline, for example, when asked about her reaction to Alice's mother, said that if she saw Alice being hit, she would just want to pull Alice out of the situation. She then went on to describe how she could never think of doing more than just getting out of the line of fire in her own family. The thought of taking further action petrified her.

SR's interventions were aimed at pointing out that the behaviors of their parents would naturally be seen as harmful when viewed in their full context and considering the kind of care parents are expected to provide. It was emphasized that it thus followed that the reactions of the group members to their parents in defense of themselves would also have to be extraordinary in some way. For example, having to keep yourself *emotionally apart* as a reaction to being hit meant, in effect, being alone in your family. SR reminded the group periodically, in expression and words, how much it hurts when people you care about and depend upon treat you badly.

SR's reaction to the discussion as a whole was to conclude that each of the individual members had had her own unique way of finding power as a child in reaction to the extreme physical discipline. She explained how it appeared that they had all found a line of defense that worked to keep themselves intact. This conceptualization led to a reconsideration of how they had reacted to their parents' violence when they were children, one that seemed to allow them to view their behavior in a much more positive light. Caroline, for example, offered (for herself and others) how their different ways of reacting—whether to fight back or in some way flee—probably each served to preserve something important inside of themselves.

*Naming the Shadows*

There was a clear recognition by the group members, by the end of the discussion, that they had, as children, been caught in the middle of something they could in no way have understood. They realized that they had thought violence was normal, and Caroline even remembered how she would defend her parents' behavior to her friends. They understood that their parents didn't recognize, in some fundamental way, what it meant to treat a child like a child, and somehow they had found the wisdom that would keep them from repeating their parents' mistakes. The following exchange illustrates the contrast of their own perspective from that of their parents. The excerpt represents continuous dialogue that has been altered only to preserve confidentiality and ensure readability. KT is the cotherapist.

*Jesse:* I remember kindergarten. My best friend at the time, Tracy, she never got hit, and it just blew my mind. I was like, "You never get hit? Your parents don't lay a hand on you?" It's like feeling like other kinds of families really do exist. (*group laughter*)

*Caroline:* My friend Bonnie had never been spanked. And I remember we had a big argument. One of the worst arguments we ever had in college was over whether children should be spanked. At the time I said, "Oh yes, definitely." Because I had to defend my parents. How could she grow up and be a nice person and never have gotten spanked? I just didn't understand that. That's what my parents told me. If you didn't get spanked, you grew up wild, like a horse that's got to be harnessed or something . . . broken. And I have people all the time tell me, you know, they say, "You don't spank Alison?" They say, "You're going to regret it." And I tell you, she behaves better than most kids I know.

*KT:* I was visiting a friend in Norway, and in Norway it is against the law to strike your child, even to spank your child.

*Caroline:* Look how small they are and how big you are. I mean, I just look at Ali. Ali thinks she can beat me up. I think it's wonderful. The only thing I've ever done to Ali physically is like, especially when she was younger, if she was going toward a direction I did not want her to go to and everything, I'd physically pick her up and put her the other way, and she would kick and scream like nothing else. *(laughter)* And I think that's normal.

*Ceci:* I think that's good too. One thing my mom and I were into when we were having our conversation is how terribly behaved Toni's children are because they were playing on the couch. And I said, "You're just totally wrong." Because Toni doesn't hit her kids and doesn't scream at them. And it's just so much nicer to be around kids that—even though they're not perfectly behaved— they at least have some creativity and the feeling they can say things. And they are just so much more in possession of themselves.

Toward the end of the discussion, the members of the group wondered, in conversation, how much perspective their mothers had about what had gone on in their family homes. They shared examples in support of the view that their mothers "didn't get it" then or now. We close with a quote from Caroline:

*Caroline:* When I told my mother that she had broken the cheeseboard on me that I had made her as a Christmas gift, spanking me, she laughed and said, "You probably deserved it." I mean, it was a *gift* I had given to her. It was a cutting board, and she spanked me with it. She used it as a paddle. I think I was in second grade.

We think Caroline was saying something profound about how families can inadvertently or otherwise take the love and dependency of their children and turn it against them.

# Afterword

There are a number of important issues concerning the psychotherapeutic treatment of adult survivors of childhood incest that we have not dealt with directly in this book, although we have commented on some implicitly. In concluding, we would simply like to call several of these issues to the attention of our readers in the hope of forecasting continued clinical interest and scholarship. All of them have been addressed within the field of traumatic stress, and the reader is referred to the *Journal of Traumatic Stress* (published by Plenum Press) and the *PTSD Research Quarterly* (published by the National Center for Post-Traumatic Stress Disorder) as excellent points of entry into the relevant literatures.

There is, of course, the so-called false memory issue. We hope that we have been clear about the pretentiousness of asserting any absolute knowledge as therapists about the life histories of the survivors whom we treat. In the process of piecing together a life narrative from the data put forward in therapy, our study members often had to confront the limits of their self-knowledge. There are ways as therapists that we can provide some comfort to survivors about this. We believe, for example, that as survivors begin to understand the meaningful place the traumatic imprint holds in their lives, there is less urgency about producing the kind of detailed accounts that fit with commonly held beliefs and narrowly focused scientific theories about memory. What we want to encourage is reliable truth seeking that comes from not cornering people into positions of certainty about those things for which they may continue to have some doubt.

We hope we have also shown our disappointment that the social or cultural context in which survivors live at this point in history does not, for the most part, encourage the same orientation toward memory that we encourage in the therapeutic context. In fact, hostile sentiments exist in our society toward survivors of childhood incest that at times seem to dominate or define the cultural constructions of traumatic memory. There is an important educational challenge for those of us who have expertise in the area of traumatic memory processes in countering dismissive and suspicious reactions now popular toward women who present themselves as having histories of childhood sexual abuse. To this end, we hope we have illustrated some of the complexities of traumatic memory in the conceptual and clinical material presented in this book.

The support of people in the communities in which survivors live, whether they be intimate partners or gatekeepers to community services, is a critical adjunct to the psychotherapy process. Survivors of childhood incest have been the victims of a failure in protection in their families. The alienation associated with the myriad psychological ramifications of this lack of protection cannot be corrected simply by the offering of psychotherapy several hours a week for a period of one year. There is clearly an important role for trauma experts in providing the kind of information and guidance that would facilitate social support.

The perpetration of abuse against children in one's family, and the failure of nonperpetrating adult family members to protect these children are societal problems of enormous proportion. To some degree they are the result of the potential for childhood maltreatment to repeat itself in generation after generation of affected families. There are, however, many survivors like the ones in our study who are extraordinary in their courage and commitment to not only break what has been called the cycle of violence, but also to generally hold to a high standard of nurturance and integrity in the treatment of all children. And though we have not highlighted the therapeutic issues for adult survivors of childhood abuse that relate to parenting, we feel strongly that this is another centrally important concern that needs further study.

The survivors about whom we have written represent models for other survivors who would like to better understand how they might live meaningful lives. We believe it is important for clinician-scholars to continue to contribute qualitative data to the literature that is informative in this way. Too often the information available on adult survivors of incest focuses solely on problems in living associated with psychological disorder and fails to celebrate any of the resiliency, heroism, or richness in these women's lives. Perhaps, too, if there were less shame and confusion surrounding the public pronouncement of having survived the sexual maltreatment by a family member, more survivors would share their life stories to the education and benefit of us all.

# References

American Psychiatric Association. (1994). *Diagnostic and statistical manual of mental disorders* (4th ed.). Washington, DC: Author.

Barlow, D., & Cerny, A. (1988). *The psychological treatment of panic*. New York: Guilford Press.

Batson, R. (1992). Multiple personality disorder: Conceptual and therapeutic resolutions. *Highland Highlights, 15,* 5–15.

——— (1994, October). *Consciousness, attachment, and the entrancement of terror.* Paper presented at the meeting of the International Society for Traumatic Stress Studies, Chicago.

Bernstein, E., & Putnam, F. (1986). Development, reliability, and validity of a dissociation scale. *Journal of Nervous and Mental Disease, 174,* 727–735.

Briere, J. (1989). *Therapy for adults molested as children: Beyond survival*. New York: Springer.

——— (1992). *Child abuse trauma: Theory and treatment of the lasting effects.* Newbury Park, CA: Sage.

Browne, A., & Finkelhor, D. (1986). Impact of child sexual abuse: A review of the research. *Psychological Bulletin, 99,* 66–77.

Cole, P. M., & Putnam, F. W. (1992). Effect of incest on self and social functioning: A developmental psychopathology perspective. *Journal of Consulting and Clinical Psychology, 60,* 174–184.

Cooley, C. H. (1902). *Human nature and the social order.* New York: Schocken Books. As excerpted in Halberstadt, A. G., and Ellyson, S. L. (Eds.). (1990). *Social psychology readings: A century of research.* New York: McGraw-Hill, pp. 61–67.

Courtois, C. (1988). *Healing the incest wound.* New York: Norton.

Csikszentmihaly, M. (1990). *Flow: The psychology of optimal experience.* New York: Harper & Row.

Davidson, J. R. T., & Foa, E. B. (Eds.). (1992). *Posttraumatic stress disorder: DSM-IV and beyond.* Washington, DC: American Psychiatric Press.

DeRosa, R. R., Roth, S., Newman, E., Pelcovitz, D., & van der Kolk, B. (1997). *Disor-*

## References

ders of extreme stress and borderline personality disorder. Manuscript submitted for publication.

Epstein, S. (1991). The self-concept, the traumatic neurosis, and the structure of personality. In D. Ozer, J. M. Healy, Jr., & A. J. Stewart (Eds.), Perspectives in personality. London: Jessica Kingsley.

——— (1994). The integration of the cognitive and the psychodynamic unconscious. American Psychologist, 49, 709–725.

Finkelhor, D., Hotaling, G., Lewis, I. A., & Smith, C. (1990). Sexual abuse in a national survey of adult men and women: Prevalence, characteristics, and risk factors. Child Abuse and Neglect, 14, 19–28.

Freud, S. (1975). Recommendations to physicians practicing psychoanalysis. In J. Strachey (Ed. and Trans.). The standard edition of the complete psychological works of Sigmund Freud (Vol. 12, pp. 109–120. London: Hogarth Press. (Original work published 1912)

Hammer, E. (1990). Reaching the affect: Style in the psychodynamic therapies. Northvale, NJ: Jason Aronson.

Havens, L. (1986). Making contact: Uses of language in psychotherapy. Cambridge: Harvard University Press.

Herman, J. L. (1992). Trauma and recovery. New York: Basic Books.

Herman, J. L., & van der Kolk, B. A. (1987). Traumatic antecedents of borderline personality disorder. In B. A. van der Kolk (Ed.), Psychological trauma. Washington, DC: American Psychiatric Press.

Horowitz, M. J. (1979). States of mind: An analysis of change in psychotherapy. New York: Plenum Press.

——— (1986). Stress response syndromes. Northvale, NJ: Jason Aronson.

Kendall-Tackett, K. A., Williams, L. M., & Finkelhor, D. (1993). Impact of sexual abuse on children: A review and synthesis of recent empirical studies. Psychological Bulletin, 113, 164–180.

Kilpatrick, D. G., Resnick, H. S., Freedy, J. R. V., Pelcovitz, D., Resick, P., Roth, S., & van der Kolk, B. (1997). The posttraumatic stress disorder field trial: Evaluation of the PTSD construct: Criteria A through E. In T. A. Widiger, A. J. Frances, H. A. Pincus, M. B. First, R. Ross, & W. Davis (Eds.), DSM-IV sourcebook (Vol. 4). Washington, DC: American Psychiatric Press.

Kluft, R. P. (Ed.). (1989). Treatment of victims of sexual abuse. Psychiatric Clinics of North America, 12, 237–503.

——— (Ed.). (1990). Incest-related syndromes of adult psychopathology. Washington, DC: American Psychiatric Press.

Lifton, N., Newman, E., Lebowitz, L., & Roth, S. (1996). The thematic adaptation measurement scale. Unpublished manuscript.

Linehan, M. M. (1993). Cognitive-behavioral treatment of borderline personality disorder. New York: Guilford Press.

Lyons, J. A., & Keane, T. M. (1989). Implosive therapy for the treatment of combat-related PTSD. Journal of Traumatic Stress, 27, 137–152.

Newman, E., Orsillo, S. M., Herman, D. S., Niles, B. L., & Litz, B. (1995). The clinical presentation of disorders of extreme stress in combat veterans. *Journal of Nervous and Mental Disease, 183,* 664–668.

Newman, E., Riggs, D., & Roth, S. (1997). Thematic resolution and PTSD: An empirical investigation of the relationships between meaning and trauma-related diagnoses. *Journal of Traumatic Stress, 10,* 197–213.

Ochberg, F. M. (1988). *Post-traumatic therapy and victims of violence.* New York: Brunner/Mazel.

Ochberg, F. M., & Willis, D. J. (Eds.). (1991). Psychotherapy with victims [Special issue]. *Psychotherapy, 28,* 1–193.

Pelcovitz, D., van der Kolk, B., Roth, S., Mandel, F. S., Kaplan, S., & Resick, P. A. (1997). Development of a criteria set and a structured interview for disorders of extreme stress (SIDES). *Journal of Traumatic Stress, 10,* 3–17.

Polusny, M. A., & Follette, V. M. (1995). Long-term correlates of child sexual abuse: Theory and review of the empirical literature. *Applied and Preventive Psychology, 4,* 143–166.

Putnam, F. W. (1989). *Diagnosis and treatment of multiple personality disorder.* New York: Guilford Press.

Reiker, P., & Carmen, R. (1986). The victim to patient process: The disconfirmation and transformation of abuse. *American Journal of Orthopsychiatry, 56,* 360–370.

Roth, S., & Batson, R. (1993). The creative balance: The therapeutic relationship and thematic issues in trauma resolution. *Journal of Traumatic Stress, 6,* 159–179.

Roth, S., DeRosa, R. R., & Turner, K. (1996). Cognitive-behavioral interventions for PTSD. In E. Giller, Jr., & L. Weiseth (Eds.), *Emerging concepts in the treatment of posttraumatic stress disorders.* London: Bailliere Tindall.

Roth, S., & Lebowitz, L. (1988). The experience of sexual trauma. *Journal of Traumatic Stress, 1,* 79–107.

Roth, S., Lebowitz, L., & DeRosa, R. (1996). Thematic assessment of posttraumatic stress reactions. In J. P. Wilson & T. M. Keane (Eds.), *Assessing psychological trauma and PTSD: A handbook for practitioners.* New York: Guilford Press.

Roth, S., & Newman, E. (1992). The role of helplessness in recovery from sexual trauma. *Canadian Journal of Behavioral Science, 24,* 220–232.

Roth, S., & Newman, E. (1993). The process of coping with incest for adult survivors: Measurement and implications for treatment and research. *Journal of Interpersonal Violence, 8* (3), 363–378. (Also reprinted in G. Everly & J. Lating (Eds.). (1995). *Psychotraumatology: Key papers and core concepts in posttraumatic stress.* New York: Plenum Press)

Roth, S., Newman, E., Pelcovitz, D., van der Kolk, B., & Mandel, F. D. (1997). Disorders of extreme stress in victims exposed to sexual and/or physical abuse: Results from the DSM-IV field trials for posttraumatic stress disorder. *Journal of Traumatic Stress* (in press).

Ruesch, J. (1966). *Therapeutic communication.* New York: Norton.

Russell, D. E. H. (1983). The incidence and prevalence of intrafamilial and extrafamilial sexual abuse of female children. *Child Abuse and Neglect, 7,* 133–146.

Saunders, B. E., Villeponteaux, L. A., Lipovsky, J. A., Kilpatrick, D. G., & Veronen, L.

References

J. (1992). Child sexual assault as a risk factor for mental health disorders among women: A community sample. *Journal of Interpersonal Violence, 7,* 189–204.

Scheibe, K. W. (1995). *Self studies: The psychology of self and identity.* Westport, CT: Praeger.

Spiegel, D. (1989). Hypnosis in the treatment of victims of sexual abuse. *Psychiatric Clinics of North America, 12,* 295–304.

Spiegel, D., & Cardena, E. (1990). New uses of hypnosis in the treatment of posttraumatic stress disorder. *Journal of Clinical Psychiatry, 51* (Suppl. 10), 39–46.

———— (1991). Disintegrated experience: The dissociative disorders revisited. *Journal of Abnormal Psychology, 100,* 366–378.

Tomkins, S. S. (1963). *Affect/imagery/consciousness: Vol. 2. The negative affects.* New York: Springer. As excerpted in Nathanson, D. L. (1992). *Shame and pride: Affect, sex, and the birth of the self.* New York: Norton, p. 146.

Turner, K., DeRosa, R., Roth, S., Batson, R., & Davidson, J. T. (1996). A multimodal treatment for incest survivors: Preliminary outcome data. *Clinical Psychology and Psychotherapy: An International Journal of Theory and Practice, 3,* 208–219.

van der Kolk, B. A. (1987). *Psychological trauma.* Washington, DC: American Psychiatric Press.

van der Kolk, B. A., Dreyfus, D., Michaels, M., Shera, D., Berkowitz, R., Fisler, R, & Saxe, G. (1994). Fluoxetine in posttraumatic stress disorder. *Journal of Clinical Psychiatry, 55,* 517–522.

van der Kolk, B., & Fisler, R. (1995). Dissociation and the fragmentary nature of traumatic memories: Overview and exploratory study. *Journal of Traumatic Stress, 8,* 505–527.

van der Kolk, B., Pelcovitz, D., Herman, J. L., Roth, S., Kaplan, S., & Spitzer, R. L. (1992). *The complicated PTSD inventory.* Unpublished manuscript.

van der Kolk, B., Pelcovitz, D., & Roth, S. (1993, October). *Disorder of extreme stress: Further analyses.* Paper presented at the ninth annual meeting of the International Society for Traumatic Stress Studies, San Antonio, TX.

van der Kolk, B., Pelcovitz, D., Roth, S., Mandel, F. S., McFarlane, A., & Herman, J. L. (1996). Dissociation, affect dysregulation and somatization. *American Journal of Psychiatry, 153,* 83–94.

World Health Organization. (1994). *The ICD-10 classification of mental and behavioural disorders with glossary and diagnostic criteria for research.* Washington, DC: American Psychiatric Press.

# Index

*Index*